COACHING 101

Guiding the High School Athlete and Building Team Success

Don Schnake

Richview Press
Elk Grove Village, Illinois

©Copyright 1996 Don Schnake
All Rights Reserved
Printed in the United States of America

This book may not be reproduced in whole or in part, by mimeograph or any other means, without permission.

Richview Press
P.O. Box 92174
Elk Grove Village, IL 60009-2174

Library of Congress Catalog Card Number: 95-71927
ISBN 0-9648738-1-8

*To Lyn, Lew, Logan, and Leigh—
You're a prideful father's dream.
You're starters on the roster
Of my all-time special team.*

Acknowledgements

This book happened because of many people. Particular thanks go to the following:

Mom and Dad—Mom only tolerated sports, but she showered me with love and taught me right from wrong—from my earliest cradle days. Dad opened my eyes to the sports world. He always found time and energy to play catch in the alley after work. And to take his wide-eyed boys to St. Louis Cardinals double-headers on steamy summer Sundays—an all day trip in the 1930s.

Teammates, coaches, teachers, and opponents—All had a hand in making me what I am.

Players and assistant coaches—No career would have happened without their efforts and loyalty over a 35-year span.

Marilyn, my buddy and my wife—Her patient and tireless determination to master publication technology helped me make the turn and cross the finish line with this project. Just as in every aspect of life, she's always there for me.

—DSS

Only he who attempts the absurd is capable of achieving the impossible.

—Miguel de Unamuno

Contents

Foreword 13
Chapter 1 Why? 17

Part I   Your Program 23

Chapter 2 Coaching's Challenge 25
Chapter 3 Philosophy and Style 29
Chapter 4 X's and O's 35
Chapter 5 Program Development 51
Chapter 6 Teaching and Motivation 67
Chapter 7 Practice 79

Part II   Relationships 93

Chapter 8 The Athletes 95
Chapter 9 The Coaching Staff 103
Chapter 10 The Classroom 109
Chapter 11 Officials 117
Chapter 12 Parents 129
Chapter 13 The Community 137
Chapter 14 College Recruiters 145
Chapter 15 The Media 151

Part III   Sundries 157

Chapter 16 Boys and Girls Together 159
Chapter 17 Getting the Job 171
Chapter 18 Godspeed! 181

Foreword

One player out of your high school conference may be lucky enough to play college ball. One college player per conference may be lucky enough to play professionally. The average pro career lasts four years. I was blessed with enough talent, positive work habits, and luck to climb that exclusive ladder and play in a championship game in all of my ten years with the Browns. I am well aware that if it hadn't been for the strength and leadership of those on the first rungs, I never would have made it off the ground.

My parents were teachers. My father was THE music department at Waukegan High in Illinois, and my mother taught piano and grade school. Over the years, hundreds of former students have told me how much my parents influenced their lives. As we get older, our memories of people fade—except for those who have touched us the most. I will never forget my high school coaches. Mark Wilson and Ralph Brown were tremendous influences, as were my college coaches, "Dutch" Lonborg and Lynn "Pappy" Waldorf.

Paul Brown shaped my life more than any other coach, and I would not be in the NFL Hall of Fame were it not for him. Paul began his career as a high school coach at

Severn Prep. He then created a dynasty at Massillon High in Ohio. His enormous success came not as the simple result of his vast knowledge of the game, but from his work ethic and common sense. His teachings off the field were as important to his boys as those learned at any practice session. Paul demanded a lot, but the results were worth the sacrifices.

As I watch the high school athletes of today, it is obvious that they are bigger, stronger, faster, and better than my peers of 60 years ago. The level of play has grown far beyond the almost sandlot quality of my time. Along with this steady growth of sport has come the need for responsible and informed professionals to nurture today's youth through the demanding task of playing ball while maintaining high academic standards. That's where this book comes in.

High school students are more physically and emotionally flexible than at any other time in their lives. Often in today's transient society, the people who have the most influence in this molding process are our teachers and coaches. It is not enough anymore to simply be able to talk X's and O's to these kids. One has to be a teacher, coach, counselor, shrink, cop, and role model all in one package.

COACHING 101 deals with areas that, until now, came only with on-the-job experience. You made your mistakes along the way and hoped for the best. Don Schnake's perceptive and practical guide brings insight and inspiration to new and veteran coaches alike. He shows how you can tend to the needs of young people, relate to others in a positive manner—and still have time to concentrate on thrashing next week's opponent.

                Otto Graham

                Football and Basketball
                All-American, 1943-44
                Northwestern University.

                Cleveland Browns QB, 1946-55
                NFL Hall of Fame, 1965

                NFL Head Coach
                Washington Redskins, 1966-68

1

Why?

Why a book about coaching high school sports? Oddly, the idea germinated in East Asia. My son Lew, a University of Maryland graduate stationed in South Korea as a member of the U.S. Air Force, had been asked to coach a high school lower level football team. And he needed help.

Responding to his plea, I discovered how much there is to tell about high school coaching—and how little is being told. Volumes describe fundamentals, techniques, and strategies of games, but few offer instruction about how to coach *people*. Countless great high school coaches spend years developing winning programs—and maintaining positive working relationships with others. But they don't write books.

A second incident sparked my drive to write. A high school administrator in Michigan requested ten copies of my book, *TROUT: The Old Man and the Orphans* and presented a copy to each of his coaches with instructions to "Read this, and see how a *real* coach does it."

The Old Man and the Orphans, written to help preserve the values and philosophies of legendary high school coach A.L. Trout, adds to the history and tradition of Illinois interscholastic athletics. Reaction from the publication indicates an interest in material to help coaches do a better job.

One side of me rebels at any notion that I should qualify for writing a book on this subject. So many others have done so much.

My other side knows, though, that beginning coaches need a practical guide for leading young athletes in today's society.

Coaching, an inexact science, has few absolutes. Thousands of brilliant coaches go about their jobs in thousands of different ways. Each is unique. Each operates with a different set of methods, philosophies, and commandments.

My name won't be found on any list of coaching immortals, but I do appreciate having a solid athletic foundation. While I cannot answer all of coaching's questions, I feel I have contributed something to four Illinois schools and communities.

Reverence for my old high school coach at Centralia, Illinois, led directly to my pursuit of a teaching and coaching career. Most of my attitudes, values, and principles stem from Mr. Trout. As my coaching conscience, his spirit guided my footsteps. Perched on my shoulder, it shuddered when I violated a cardinal rule—and nodded approval when something went right.

Arthur Trout personified the positive aspects of athletics within the educational experience. Moreover, he did it with color, drama, and vivid imagination. And he won games. In basketball alone, he produced 809 victories, ten state tournament teams, and three state titles. On the way to accumulating 65 championship trophies, he influenced thousands of young people on the court, on the field, and in the classroom. Renowned as a sportsman of the highest order, Trout mixed innovation, showmanship, and phenomenal success with old-fashioned values, down-to-earth humility, and delightful eccentricities. He was an outright original—a beacon light of integrity and scholarship among his peers. Playing for Mr. Trout was a blessing, and I will refer to him many times throughout this book.

As a schoolboy athlete, I competed against teams of such Illinois coaching greats as Harry Combes, Stan

Changnon, Ernie Eveland, Gay Kintner, Dolph Stanley, and Duster Thomas.

My collegiate years included one season with the Bradley Braves basketball team. During that time, Bradley dominated the national rankings and finished the 1949-50 campaign as runners-up in both the National Invitation Tournament and the NCAA Finals.

The Bradley experience provided rich opportunities to learn from outstanding teammates—including All-Americans Paul Unruh and Gene Melchiorre—as well as from many of the country's best players at college basketball's highest level. I was also privileged to study at close range the methods of such storied coaching figures as Phog Allen, Clair Bee, Eddie Hickey, Nat Holman, Henry Iba, Frank McGuire, Ray Meyer, and Adolph Rupp.

More significantly, I developed a sensitivity to players' feelings that led me to embrace human dignity as a core issue in my coaching philosophy.

As a young Illinois high school assistant, I became a disciple of two outstanding and respected men—Merv Baker of Charleston and George Pratt of Aledo.

As a head coach, I attended coaching clinics and visited college campuses to enrich my background. Listening to and talking with people such as Alex Agase, George Allen, Frank Broyles, Bear Bryant, Woody Hayes, Lou Holtz, John

McKay, Ara Parseghian, Joe Paterno, Eddie Robinson, John Robinson, Darrell Royal, Bo Schembechler, Bill Walsh, Bud Wilkinson and Bowden Wyatt gave inspiration and enlightenment. At a clinic at the University of Colorado during the middle '50s, Coach John Wooden provided a lifetime memory by sharing a soft drink and answering a mountain of my coaching questions during a lengthy private discussion.

Through the years, dedicated assistant coaches and faithful friends have contributed invaluable advice and suggestions. Brendan Flynn—the classic model of a loyal assistant and priceless friend—stands at the front of this long line of steadfast allies.

My purpose in writing this book is to share observations and opinions culled from nearly 60 years of watching, listening, reading, and doing. Younger readers, or those from different geographic areas, may recognize few of the names found on the following pages. It makes little difference. These are true people who shaped my athletic thinking during my time and in my part of the country. Their attitudes and beliefs carry just as much relevance today as they did then. Maybe more.

It's the sort of simple book—written in clear mother tongue—I'd want my sons, daughters, or grandchildren to read should they ever want to coach. Please be patient with occasional clichéd comments. The sporting world communicates in its own peculiar way.

And so, in an informal style to create a comfortable climate, I volunteer counsel and encouragement to those young men and women who seek the title of *Coach*—and to those already in the field who wish to become better at what they do.

Many mistakes marred my rewarding and often scary career. I offer to you the advice I wish someone had given *me* as I thrashed about during those early years. These are hard lessons learned about things that count.

To borrow a line heard at nearly every coaching clinic, "If you can pick up just one good idea here, your time has been well spent."

Part I

Your Program

2

Coaching's Challenge

So you want to coach!

Coaching has always been hard work. Today, it's staggering. A person must have a *compulsion* to coach and teach. Yesterday's schools battled teenagers over gum-chewing, noise-making, and hallway mischief. Modern schools contend with alcohol and drug abuse, assault, pregnancy, rape, robbery, and suicide. Teachers no longer just teach. They counsel, doctor, nurse, parent, and protect. And coaches do more.

With greater opportunities to enjoy other activities, many youngsters choose to bypass athletics. We *expect* growing urban problems to cut into city athletic programs.

But we are baffled when a small-town Michigan high school's football season evaporates in mid-stride. Reason? Its players simply lost the wish to play.

Most experienced coaches see today's athletes as being more difficult to handle than the competitors of a few years back. Young people watch television and see great athletes showboat, flout fundamentals, and taunt opponents. Many of today's youngsters contest discipline, resent hard work, and resist motivation. Athletes' noxious attitudes and lack of respect drive coaches away from every sport on every competition level.

We hear of school administrators overruling coaches' disciplinary measures as they buckle under parental or community pressures.

Even high school coaches cheapen the integrity and image of interscholastic sports when they illegally recruit players from other schools. Grade-tampering scandals continue to rock inner-city programs. Coaches make headlines when they allow scholastically ineligible athletes to play. And a school makes headlines when it permits a basketball player to participate for four years—and then disallows graduation because of poor grades.

Although problem parents have been around for years, their numbers increase as their voices grow louder.

Faulty assessment of their children's abilities leads to unrealistic expectations. They demand starting assignments, reams of flattering publicity, postseason recognition, and college scholarships. And the team must win.

Grandstand critics and second-guessers (experts through television and radio) vocalize louder and more often today. Radio and television commentators earn handsome wages—often following network demands to "go after" coaches and players. Newspaper columnists entertain their readers with controversy, color, and criticism. And even conscientious reporters often fail to see how professional and college games and athletes differ from their high school counterparts.

The most ideal coaching situations still call for extraordinary time commitment. Nearly all sports have evolved into year-round undertakings with off-season training camps, summer leagues, weight-training programs, and fundraising expectations. Meanwhile, school administrators continue to push for their coaches to become more involved in classroom work.

Discouraged? Chin up.

Recently, a major metropolitan newspaper detailed complaints by several high school coaches who grumbled loudest about being underpaid for their coaching duties. But the following day, that same paper featured an article describing a young man who had given up a six figure salary in the corporate world to become a high school teacher and coach.

Some contend that building successful athletic programs may be even easier today. While numbers may be smaller than before, many young men and women are still willing to commit themselves to hard work and dedication to a cause. When they find a coach who can inspire and direct—and knows how to win—they will follow.

Young people need someone to care about them outside the classroom. Take inventory of your personal qualities. Successful coaches are:

- competitive.
- consistent.
- honest.
- knowledgeable.
- passionate.
- persistent.
- positive.
- proud.
- resilient.
- secure.
- tough.
- confident.
- determined.
- industrious.
- patient.
- people-smart.
- poised.
- prepared.
- reliable.
- resourceful.
- strong-willed.
- visionary.

Measure up?

If you've got the moxie—and a star you have to follow—take a shot. Commit yourself to excellence, and dedicate yourself to coaching. Step into a world filled with exhilarating victory, depressing defeat, and a challenge every minute.

3

Philosophy and Style

As seasoned travelers plot the route of a long journey, prospective coaches must chart their paths to success. Even those who have been on the trail for years should occasionally step back and take stock of their direction.

Philosophy and style are your map and compass. A philosophy is the sum of one's fundamental attitudes, beliefs, and values. How you go about implementing your philosophy becomes your style. All coaches have philosophies and styles of operation—though they often do so unconsciously. Philosophy and style—difficult to separate—intertwine and influence each other. Philosophy determines style; style reflects philosophy.

- As a coach, where are you now?
- Where do you want to be?
- How do you intend to get there?
- How important is winning to you?
- Where does nurturing the growth of young men and women fit into your set of principles?
- Does fun have a place in your idea of coaching?

Nothing quite matches winning's euphoria. We all want to win. Keeping your job may depend upon winning an acceptable number of games. If winning were not important, we wouldn't need scoreboards.

Perhaps a bigger question is, "When does important become too important?" Vince Lombardi's notorious quotation that "Winning isn't everything, it's the only thing" has triggered endeavors to win at all costs at all levels. Coaches from Pop Warner Leagues to the NFL have adopted his statement as gospel. He spoke those words, however, to professional football players and to business corporations in motivational speeches. In both cases, winning means money; money means success. Is winning games the only thing in high school sports?

Disciples of the "Winning is the only thing" philosophy may:
- play ill, injured, or ineligible players.
- alter transcripts.

- falsify birth dates.
- encourage or initiate transfers.
- permit or encourage taunting.
- bait game officials.
- spy on opposing teams.
- suggest diuretics to "make weight."

After a 54-year history—checkered by falsification of birth certificates and residence records, plus abuse and violence toward umpires, players, parents, coaches, and fans—Little League recorded its first homicide in 1993. Following a game in California, racial trash talk kindled a melee that resulted in a player being fatally struck by a baseball bat.

When it comes to winning, where will you draw *your* line?

Where does looking after the growth of young men and women fit into your philosophy? Responsibility for athletes' physical, emotional, and social development is astounding. Your every word, deed, and expression can become indelible. For good or bad, you *will* affect young athletes.

Is there a place in your philosophy for fun? We read and hear about coaches making practices and games enjoyable. Their athletes have fun while competing. Others claim that tough competition is too demanding, and locker room victory celebrations are the only fun part of athletics.

Coaching styles vary. Many associate success

(winning) with such hard-shelled authoritarians as Bear Bryant, George Halas, Woody Hayes, and Vince Lombardi. They left mercy to heaven.

At the opposite extreme, John Gagliardi, who coaches college football at tiny St. John's of Minnesota reportedly:

- cuts no players.
- holds no staff meetings.
- uses no slogans.
- permits teams to practice in shorts or sweats.
- allows no sleds, dummies, laps, or wind sprints.
- ridicules calisthenics.
- takes a laissez-faire stance toward weight training.
- keeps no statistics.
- uses no whistle.
- does no off-campus recruiting.
- allows no contact drills during practices.
- uses no playbooks or film.
- permits his quarterbacks to select the plays.

Can you coach this way and still win? Gagliardi joins Eddie Robinson, Bear Bryant, Amos Alonzo Stagg, and Pop Warner as the only college coaches to collect more than 300 victories.

Between these extremes, thousands of others have enjoyed great success while following different philosophies and using a variety of coaching methods.

When you select a philosophy or coaching style,

remember that modern coaching methods differ from those of yesteryear. Blindly follow an old-fashioned autocratic style of coaching in today's environment, and you make a major mistake. But there's still a place for the hard-nosed approach that accepts nothing less than total dedication and all-out effort—a *play the damn defense* mentality. Kids still want to be *coached*.

The careers of most coaching giants from earlier eras spanned several decades. To survive, they learned to adjust to changing times without compromising their basic beliefs. Outstanding coaches from the past would be equally great today. Coaching in the '90s, the old masters would be just as demanding—but more diplomatic.

Your philosophy will govern every decision you make and every action you take. You believe as you do because of principles acquired from your home, school, church, neighborhood, and playground. Your basic character may have been influenced by others, but you have the power to modify your outlook by reading, watching, and listening.

How important is sportsmanship? Honesty?

How will you approach winning and losing?

How will you motivate?

How will you relate with:

- players?

- coaches?
- teachers?
- administrators?
- officials?
- parents?
- fans?
- the media?

My philosophy? Teach individuals and teams to play hard, smart, and clean. Build a strong sportsmanship ethic. Push for perfection, and winning will follow. Care about people. Care and be fair.

You need to understand your own philosophy—and you need to do it now. Job interviews will examine how you see coaching's place in the education process. What's your view on how things should be done in athletics? Develop your philosophy; and stick with it. Make the right way become your way.

4

X's and O's

Successful coaches see the importance of behavior patterns, motivation methods, communication skills, public relations principles, and teaching techniques. But the real fun of coaching comes from teaching the game. Knowledge of your game is vital to earning respect and credibility. When players detect a lack of acumen, they quickly lose trust. School administrators, fans, parents, and the media also expect coaches to know their business.

Previous playing experience, while not mandatory, can be a great advantage in forming a fundamental appreciation of the game and understanding athletes' mentalities. Those who have played know what it takes. They've been there.

But having been an outstanding performer can also be

a liability. Gifted athletes often fail to understand why other athletes cannot duplicate their skills. Many times, star players find it difficult to relate to average athletes and fail as coaches when they become intolerant of mediocrity.

Yet, some find success without having played. A passionate attachment to the game and a zeal to succeed can overcome the handicap of non-participation. Studying the game in great depth and using the fundamentals of *people-skills*—abilities, talents, and techniques of effectively dealing with people—can bring positive results.

Max Kurland amassed more than 600 victories during an exceptional 35-year career as basketball coach at Chicago's St. Patrick High School. He never played high school or college basketball.

James "Barney" Oldfield, a non-athlete in high school and college, began his brief basketball coaching career as an assistant at Davenport (Iowa) High School. After two years and two sophomore conference titles, he became head coach at McKendree College in Illinois, where his teams won conference championships in each of his six years at the helm.

While admitting that a non-playing background can be detrimental, Oldfield maintains that the advantages clearly outweigh the handicaps.

He trained himself to become a keen observer. He was

so obsessed with the game that he developed a scientist's stubborn curiosity and sought the *real* truths about the game of basketball—not what *seemed* to be true.

"As a virgin in the athletic world," says Oldfield, "I carried no burdens of ego-identity. No suppositions to pass on to others. No systems to perpetuate. My natural skepticism uncovered numerous sacred basketball concepts that turned out to be nothing more than pure hooey."

Oldfield believes young men or women with no playing experience face a stacked deck. Yet, if they have exceptional desire, they can do it.

Most good coaches combine a background of modest athletic talent with a genuine love of sports. They have been average enough to feel compassion for those with limited abilities—and respect for those with superior skills. They have succeeded enough to be confident; they have failed enough to be humble.

Regardless of your experience, you can't sit back with smug confidence. You don't have all the answers. Games continually evolve. Stay abreast of the changes. Professional growth never stops.

An important breakthrough in athletic preparation during the past 30 years has been the evolution of weight-training programs to improve athletic execution and to reduce injuries. Before getting caught up in offensive and defensive theories, fundamental skill techniques, or team strategies, the modern coach must recognize that stronger bodies perform more efficiently. Every athlete in every sport benefits from proper weight training. Girls have also joined the race to become bigger, faster, and stronger.

Self-improvement programs stir interest in an increasing number of high schools. Proponents contend that these sessions are beginning to do for mental attitudes what weight training has been doing for bodies. They claim that youngsters who take part become more disciplined, positive, confident, and relaxed as they experience growth in self-esteem. *Visualization*—forming positive mental images of successful athletic performance—is a major element of these projects.

Improvements in the complex area of mental attitudes—unlike physical gains—are harder to confirm. Many schools, however, do report that athletes raise grade point averages after participating in the programs.

Coaches must recognize the magnitude of the mental side of sports performance and be alert to new methods of progression in this vital aspect.

Coaching clinics monitor the pulse of change as they offer new ideas on schemes, techniques, and theories. But veteran coaches caution that clinic attendance can be the most perilous time in a young coach's life. The danger lies in becoming "sold" on one intriguing notion after another. You'll be as tempted as a two-year-old near a mud puddle. Only iron willpower can keep you from jumping in with both feet.

Select clinics with speakers and topics of greatest interest and benefit. Occasionally, as older coaches become locked into their convictions, they seem to learn nothing at clinics. Many times, though, the value of a clinic is having one's beliefs validated by a different source.

Clinics also offer opportunities to network by talking shop with fellow coaches. More ideas change hands on napkins in coffee shops and bars than in lecture halls. Put aside feelings of intimidation. Never hesitate to seek advice from more experienced coaches. Search out others. Form friendships. Share. Learn.

Early in my career, George Pratt of Aledo offered a valuable tip for attending clinics and informal gab sessions. "Talk to teach—but listen to learn."

If you choose wisely and attend intelligently, every clinic will help you become a better coach.

Coaches have the reputation of sharing ideas—to a point. But time restraints limit comprehensive treatment of materials presented at clinics. They say a little knowledge can be dangerous. Get the rest of the story.

To further explore ideas discovered at a clinic, spend time on campus. This is where to pick up the nuts and bolts. Build relationships with coaches in high quality programs. Become identified with people who personify your ideals. By associating with successful and respected coaches, you will supplement your knowledge and maintain contacts that may help advance your career. Those in educational circles refer to this concept as *mentoring*. Most college staffs welcome high school coaches. Frequent visits by those with sincere interest lead to more open sharing.

Books, magazines, and newspapers provide further opportunities to keep current. Technological advancements in videotape and VCR machines offer a grand avenue to examine the latest trends and techniques. Increasing numbers of televised games make it easy to tape and study teams with styles similar to yours.

In coaching team sports, select a definite system of play for each season. This is crucial. Never alter offensive and defensive schemes—once in place—without long and deep thought.

Change wastes time invested in learning. Equally precious time must then be spent in mastering a new system. Minor adjustments are always necessary, but your credibility suffers with each major change. Every deviation points to original error—or to wavering resolve. Be a leader—not a windsock.

One theory holds that talent determines the style of play. To install a complex and sophisticated pro-style passing attack with a mediocre quarterback and sub-par receivers would be folly. To insist that a team of Clydesdales rely on the fast break in a racehorse brand of basketball would be equally foolish.

Most high school coaches cannot recruit, draft, or trade to stock the right talent to support an extreme style of play. Consider a basic system with enough flexibility to adapt to your personnel. Many good coaches adjust when their players don't fit their favorite system.

Don Shula, as a professional coach, enjoyed the luxury of drafting and trading players. Yet he won more football games than any other coach in NFL history by recognizing personnel abilities and altering his system accordingly.

In the '50s and '60s, Coach Shula blended the talents of players like Alan Ameche, Raymond Berry, John Mackey, Tom Matte, Lenny Moore, and John Unitas into balanced Baltimore Colt units that won NFL titles.

During the '70s, Larry Csonka, Jim Kiick, and Mercury Morris led a relentless ground assault that produced back-to-back Super Bowl victories and a perfect 17-0 season for the Miami Dolphins. Quarterback Bob Griese rarely passed the football more than ten times per game.

Shula has used Dan Marino's passing magic to propel the Dolphins to Super Bowl XIX—and on into the '90s.

Advice gathered from many seasons in the field:

- Build a simple system with balance.
- Avoid extremes.
- Maximize importance of defense.

Young coaches share an obsession with scoring and tend to emphasize offensive play. Veterans know that success in all team sports—and many individual sports—lies with strong, sound, aggressive, and inspired defensive play. They survive the big games by preventing opponents from winning. Meanwhile, their offenses cobble together a way to reach victory. Make defense the rock you build your team on.

The system's scope must be narrow enough to allow its mastery within the limits of available practice time—yet wide enough to cover every possible situation.

Any style can be successful. There is no best way. A series of matchups between two southern Illinois high school basketball powers in the '40s and '50s illustrates this point.

The programs were philosophic opposites. The tiny town of Pinckneyville counted bituminous coal and Duster

Thomas as its most valuable resources. Young boys, when asked by elementary teachers about their ambitions in life, commonly expressed the dream of playing basketball for Coach Thomas—and then working the mines.

Thomas earned his status as a basketball legend by winning a state championship with a sinking, clogging, zone-like man-to-man defense, rugged rebounding, and a methodical, patient, and percentage-conscious offense.

Centralia, some 40 miles away, relied on an aggressive defense with full-court pressure and an alert transition offense. The games featured sellout crowds, state tournament stakes, and nail-biting drama.

The opposing coaches—a pair of hidebound mavericks—shared equal measures of success, because they:

- believed in their systems.
- understood their systems.
- sold their systems.
- taught their systems.
- never changed their systems.

One coaching approach is to play as hard as possible—and emphasize doing the right things at the right times in the right ways. The degree of fundamental perfection determines the likelihood of victory.

*Fight the fight with all your might
To put trophies on the shelf.
Make every play in the proper way,
And winning takes care of itself.*

Prepare for the *game* rather than gear up for specific opponents. Tournament play—the critical part of the schedule when teams either fly or die—allows scant time for preparing and practicing special schemes for special teams.

According to his UCLA players, Coach Wooden never mentioned winning or beating another team. Coach Trout always stressed competing against the game. Neither man believed in scouting basketball teams or individual players. They were not about to change anything. Why scout?

The popularity of postseason football playoffs has led to increased emphasis on schemes with enough elasticity to attack generic rather than specific opponents.

Some successful football coaches complete an entire season with as few as six basic running plays and a simple passing attack. This package allows sufficient practice repetitions to guarantee near-perfect execution and leaves enough time to work on variations, gadget plays, defense, and the kicking game. For further coverage of this topic, see *FOOTBALL'S SIMPLE SIX: Building an Aggressive,*

Efficient, and Explosive High School Football Offense by Don Schnake, Richview Press.

At the same time, be cautious of becoming too simplistic. Players, properly motivated, may be capable of perfecting a system beyond your expectations. Find that magic area between "too little" and "too much" that matches the ability, intelligence, and hunger of your team.

For every great coach who adapts a system to fit players' abilities, another great one persists in perfecting a proven style and then molding the players to fit the system. Lists of successful coaches include numerous devotees of repetition and execution (as opposed to trickery and deception). Many run the same plays for years. And they do it with a swagger that says, "This is what we do; let's see you stop it!"

Pat Harmon, in his *Champaign News-Gazette* column, detailed how Fred Corray, former Illinois high school football coach at Salem, volunteered to help prepare the Urbana team for their 1938 game with Centralia. Corray knew all the plays and tendencies of Coach Trout, because Salem had long been Centralia's most bitter rival.

Corray placed special stress on stopping Centralia's favorite play. When a particular spread formation appeared, the fullback would invariably run into the center of the line on a delayed buck. Under Corray's instruction, a practice squad ran the play repeatedly all week against the Urbana defense.

The turning point of Centralia's landslide victory came on the first play from scrimmage. Trout's team lined up in the expected spread formation. Fullback Sam Mooney took the snap, delayed, and bolted straight up the middle for a 70-yard touchdown run.

Trout also weathered four decades of basketball evolution and never changed his defensive scheme. Early in his career, he adopted a single defense—one that could be used in all situations. He then taught it with absolute thoroughness.

He created a relentless full-court switching man-to-man with zone principles. His teams pressed all game, every game. Mastery of the defense began in the sixth grade.

Centralia High School produced an extraordinary number of state champion and medalist high jumpers during Trout's career. All the jumpers were basketball players, and some experts theorized that six or seven years of crouching and sprinting while playing the withering pressure defense developed those muscles used to high jump.

Ralph Tasker, the enormously successful high school basketball coach at Hobbs, New Mexico, uses another version of a blistering full-court press that never changes.

Today's basketball experts may reject such a theory of defense as being out of vogue and too timeworn to control the modern offenses. This may be true. But how can you discount Trout's 809 victories and those of Tasker (over 1,000 and counting)?

John Chaney, basketball coach at Temple University, preaches constant repetition of one simple system. He explains why he gives his players—and himself—no way out. "You got to make it work when you only got one."

At least one other current basketball guru follows the old-fashioned philosophy. Pat Riley, who earned four world championship rings while coaching the Los Angeles Lakers has said, "I've learned this about the playoffs. You don't make adjustments. You make players more aggressive. Play your basic game—but with greater intensity. If you're not good enough at what you do after eight months...then you're just not good enough."

Riley, chosen as the 1993 NBA Coach of the Year for his work with the New York Knicks, perhaps developed this concept while playing college ball for Adolph Rupp. Coach Rupp, the Baron of Kentucky, allegedly sent his Wildcat playbook to new rival coaches. Is this arrogance?

Win through execution.

As you assemble your collection of X's and O's, make choices that fit your comfort level. Base your selection of a playing style on experience and familiarity. For instance, if I were choosing a system of basketball defense to contain today's offenses, I would select a tough, confrontational, full-court, switching man-to-man. Why?

- It can be used in all situations.
- Its track record is proven.
- I understand it better.

Conceding to concerns regarding modernization and diversification, I would supplement the press I know with a system of traps, double-teams, and rotation patterns borrowed from the professional game and top college programs. Having a limited understanding of these techniques and tactics, I would exhaust every avenue to build a relationship with the best coaches who use a similar system. And I would create opportunities to gain insight into their defensive schemes. Then I would tailor these techniques to fit my system of defense for the high school level.

I would help motivate my defenders and rebounders by installing a statistic popularized by the Chicago Bulls. Players earn a point each time they touch the basketball while playing defense or rebounding.

Finally, using visualization, I would challenge them to play defense and rebound with the fury of a pack of cut-loose watchdogs.

Reputations, once acquired, cling to coaches like

beggar's lice to bird dogs. As a football coach, I worshiped the running game, play-action passes, a ferocious defense, and a soundly taught kicking game. We stressed clock-control, flawless execution, field position, and—most of all—being in the proper frame of mind to get these things done.

As we left the field after a big victory in which our quarterback passed for more than 200 yards and three touchdowns, a fan complained by asking why our team *ran* all the time.

We sold our players on an offense more like a freight train than a high-wire act. Rival coaches joked that we shunned summer passing leagues, because we were too busy searching for a half-line off-tackle league. Relying on our image, we wasted no time establishing the run and used play-action passing from the opening snap.

Once, as we prepared to confront a team with vastly superior talent, we looked at the facts. This team's defenders had not only crushed opponents' ground attacks, but their terrorizing pass rush had left a trail of mentally devastated and physically injured quarterbacks.

With our small number of running plays and pass patterns, we discovered we could run most of our package from a shotgun formation with only minor assignment adjustments. During the week, we spent our offensive time perfecting the direct snap and timing our plays.

Our rivals, knowing that we would be running, never fully recovered from the trauma of suddenly facing a barrage of passes from the shotgun set. Although we lost the game, our quarterback completed three touchdown passes and was never sacked. Ironically, we felt in postgame retrospect that more running from the spread formation should have brought victory.

What appeared to be junking one system for another in just four practice days was, in reality, a minor adjustment within our basic scheme.

Settle on a system. Create your own identity. Become known for *something*. Learn all you can from others, but follow your own path. Experience is the only trustworthy teacher.

5

Program Development

A program is a system of approach toward an objective. As a head coach, you lead your athletic program by determining through your priorities which elements are relevant. What must be done? How must it be done? Why must it be done? You show the way by guiding the behaviors of your staff and players.

Learn all you can about leadership. Study history's leaders. Examine the qualities that great leaders share. What characteristics allow these people to direct their followers toward goals or results? As an example, no reading list for leadership would be complete without including Alfred Lansing's *Endurance*—the incredible story of Sir Ernest

Shackleton's Imperial Trans-Antarctic Expedition.

Think of your program as a closed corporation with relatively few stockholders. The stock is not publicly traded. You head the corporation; assistant coaches and players hold the stock. Your responsibility as corporate head is to guarantee that no element of the program carries a higher priority than your athletes' welfare.

UNITY

Develop a mindset that you, your coaches, and your athletes forge a bond in a common quest for excellence. Such a union becomes interlocked more tightly as players and coaches build mutual respect. When head coaches, assistant coaches, and players share high expectations of each other and show a willingness to sacrifice personal gain for the common good, they begin building a healthy relationship. Teach your players to play for each other. Devote time and effort to strengthen this bond. The quality of player-to-player, coach-to-player, player-to-coach, and coach-to-coach linkages will determine your level of success. Group spirit can generate infinite powers.

Coaches who have been great players often lack sensitivity toward the reserve members of their squads. In their drive for perfection, they may rivet their concentration on the ones who play the most—and neglect the substitutes.

Build a strong team concept. Backup players practice just as hard as the starters; they sacrifice as much; they care as much. And they do so without the glory of the game night spotlight.

See to it that all team members get playing time at every opportunity. Aside from the ethics question of running up scores during one-sided victories, failure to substitute freely is criminal and heartless. Build positive self-esteem in your bench; don't destroy it.

Make a habit of giving attention and encouragement to those less talented. These players comprise a vital part of your program. Why keep it a secret? Go out of your way to guarantee that all players feel they are important members of the team. Treat the best players and the least gifted with the same respect and dignity.

Strengthen the team concept by minimizing individual recognition. Permit no altering of team uniforms or wearing them in a manner that draws attention to specific players. We call them uniforms for a reason. Uniform means *the same*. Many successful coaches believe in selecting captains, presenting helmet decals for special accomplishments, creating weekly individual awards, etc. While these schemes seem to work for them, my comfort level has been best served by limiting individual honors to required traditional postseason presentations—such as Most Valuable Player. Limit the number of awards, and select the recipients by team vote.

Coach Charlie Spoonhour delighted his St. Louis University basketball squad by naming the entire roster as being most valuable at the team's annual awards banquet in 1994. Each player, including two redshirts, received MVP plaques.

Coaches' philosophies regarding presentation of varsity letters range from simple specific participation requirements to elaborate point systems based upon:

- faithfully attending practice sessions.
- obeying all team rules.
- attending off-season strength and agility programs.
- participating in summer camps and leagues.
- serving at fundraising events.
- achieving academic honors.

Players contribute to team success in many ways beyond game participation. To retain team membership, all players must play their roles. Award a school letter to every team member. Each deserves a memento in return for sacrifices and contributive efforts. Critics contend that this practice cheapens the varsity letter's value. Let your conscience make your choice.

Coach Tasker has won more than 1000 basketball games by doing such things as recognizing the value of team morale. He traditionally starts every player on the roster at least one game each season.

We've all heard the term *players' coach*. These coaches work at making players feel important by talking to them and listening to them—individually and as a team. Players have a stake in the team. They pay their dues, and they deserve to be informed and aware. Be close with them without becoming anybody's best buddy.

Meaningful time spent together breeds stronger relationships. A.L. Trout conducted early morning shooting sessions for his basketball teams throughout the school year. These voluntary practices sharpened shooting skills and led to opportunities for discussing a variety of topics.

Trout often interrupted shooting drills to herd his boys into a nearby classroom. There, he reviewed articles from coaching publications, evaluated pertinent newspaper accounts, and lectured on the most current ideas regarding nutrition, rest, and cleanliness. He molded mental attitudes by stressing the importance of academic excellence, good citizenship, strong moral values, and the dignity of hard work. He defined good sportsmanship and laid out expectations for conduct around school, around town, and toward opponents and game officials. He discussed any subject at any time if it benefited individuals or the athletic program.

Trout read letters from former players who praised the program, urged players to do their best, and thanked their old coach for making high school the best days of their lives. During World War II, the letters took on a more emotional tone as they streamed in from all parts of the globe.

Centralia began all trips to away games immediately at the end of the school day. Regardless of the trip's length, no player went home or elsewhere after school on a travel day. Trout provided pregame and postgame meals during every trip. Besides ensuring proper rest and diet by monitoring all pregame activities, he established the desired mental and emotional atmosphere for the evening.

Your situation may not permit morning practices. Elements of today's society compete for greater amounts of players' time. Your school and community may have a passive athletic tradition. Your budget may not allow for team meals.

Although parts of your program may fall short of being ideal, recognize the benefits of togetherness in helping to cement the unity of your squad. Search for ways to become close—and stay that way.

During one of my coaching assignments, a change in

pastors at our family church led to a series of unusual bonding experiences. The new minister, an avid football fan, became a frequent observer at our practices. Wishing to vitalize his new congregation, the parson invited the squad to visit one of his services. With the clear understanding that individual attendance would be completely voluntary, the group voted to accept the offer.

Representing a wide range of faiths, the entire team—scrubbed clean and radiating pride—sat beaming on that sunny Sunday morning.

Word travels fast in small towns. Other denominations beckoned, and we brightened the corner of a different church each week for the remainder of the season.

Attending church services as a group proved to be a positive for our situation. Careful, though. Religious beliefs and public education make a combustible combination. Don't play with fire.

Looking back, we believe that attitudes of the town, the players, and their parents meshed at a time that had to be right for this to work. And a two-year record of 17-1 in a town that wasn't used to winning didn't hurt. Nevertheless, those few Sundays of long ago provided indelible memories for a team of players and hundreds of proud-spirited churchgoers.

DISCIPLINE

What is discipline? Many equate discipline with tyranny and punishment for breaking rules. Coaches labeled as strict disciplinarians (once a complimentary description) have lost favor and are now looked upon as tyrants.

Look at discipline in a more positive light. Discipline is training to establish and perfect desired behavior patterns, mental attitudes, and moral character.

Begin by disciplining yourself to develop and maintain a sharp fixation on precisely what you want and exactly where you want to go. Then teach and motivate your players to achieve identically clear concentration.

Instill discipline in your team through an explicit focus on the use of proper measures in the proper manner at the proper time. And doing it all the time.

Everybody wants to win on Friday night, but life's winners do the necessary little things during the week that prepare themselves for the big game. To illustrate this point, recognize that coaching defensive basketball goes far beyond instruction in mechanical fundamentals. The real key lies in developing your players' character to the point where they have the resolve and competitive fiber to put aside glamour and accept the dirty work of diving for loose balls, playing tough team defense, and rebounding.

This concept of discipline as educational outgrowth is nothing new. In 1887, Thomas Huxley, the noted British naturalist and writer, said, "Perhaps the most valuable result of all education is the ability to make yourself do the thing you have to do when it ought to be done, *whether you like it or not.* It is the first lesson that should to be learned, and however early a man's training begins, it is probably the *last* lesson that he learns thoroughly."

Being punctual and accepting responsibility on a daily basis will make better players, better teams, and more productive citizens in life beyond the athletic world. You have a unique opportunity—an obligation—to instill beneficial lifelong habits.

TRAINING RULES

In earlier times, training rules fell under the domain of the head coach—the voice of law and order. Acting with sovereignty, the coach made the rules, interpreted the rules, and enforced the rules.

Today, most city and suburban school administrators either formulate proper training procedures or share policy-making with coaches. The growing number of athletic teams has created the need for consistency. Schools often include all extracurricular activities in their behavior codes.

Regardless of who makes them, the rules should be simple, clear, and few. Hard rules and threatened punishments can become recipes for disaster. Leave yourself room. In the '90s, coaches may be more effective as counselors than as dictators. Some have success with honor systems and pledge codes, but there are no guarantees.

Many Wisconsin schools use a self-reporting system. Players, team captains, and parents pledge to report training infractions. The principal of a Milwaukee High School shocked the entire state by accusing 20 parents of covering up their children's involvement in a beer party after they had signed agreements forms.

Most parents honor the codes they sign. Some disregard the law and the school's attempt to address the issues of physical and moral well-being when they chaperone drinking parties in their homes. They reason, senselessly, that teenagers will find a way to drink, anyway.

Most school leaders regard alcohol abuse as their top problem. Others fight the drug culture. While tobacco use appears to be fading in our society, smoking rates among high schoolers continue to rise. The results of a recent government survey indicate a stunning resurgence of marijuana use among teenagers—nearly doubling since 1992—after dropping steadily during each of the previous 13 years. Talk of steroid use by high school athletes has quietly diminished over the past decade. The expanding number of giant football players, though, generates suspicion that some have taken shortcuts to become bigger, faster, and stronger. Be alert to dramatic gains in size and strength. Counsel your players about long-range health risks. As long as kids want to excel in sports—and look good doing it—they face temptation.

The United States Supreme Court entered the training rules picture in 1995, when it ruled—by split decision—that public schools may make athletes submit to random drug tests. Mixed reactions by administrators, coaches, athletes, and parents greeted the ruling. Controversy swirls around singling out athletes, excluding alcohol testing, and infringing on privacy rights. Regardless of morality issues, the practical aspect of money availability takes precedence. Most school districts, already short of cash to operate athletic programs, will find testing to be too expensive. In the end, decisions to test or not to test will be made by local school systems.

Society's growing crime rate involving young people adds more problems for schools and coaches as they formulate disciplinary codes of conduct for students and student-athletes. The situation raises questions.

- Should an athlete continue to participate after being accused of committing a crime?

- Would banning an athlete before a conviction deny that athlete's constitutional rights?
- Should a felony be treated differently than a misdemeanor crime?
- How many chances should an athlete get?

School codes and coaches' philosophies vary. Some allow participation while they work with violators to help them adjust their lives. Others follow the letter of the law (those accused are innocent until proven guilty). Most take a harder line (those who make the program look bad are gone).

Know your community, your school, and your athletes. Your experiences as a player and your own personal moral values will help determine your attitude concerning appropriate behaviors.

After you have established the rules, share them with your superiors and clearly explain them to your players. It is vital that the athletes understand your expectations—and the consequences for noncompliance. Be prepared to back up your rules. Again, your credibility is on the line.

Just as you motivate your players to improve their skill execution and their game performance, inspire them to comply with behavior regulations. Convince them that using alcohol, tobacco, or drugs is unhealthy, dangerous, and illegal. Such use is just plain wrong—and it will not be tolerated. Ultimately, this may be your most significant coaching accomplishment. You can influence the course of your athletes' lives. And you just may save your job. Coaches have been fired by taking too much—or too little—disciplinary action.

Some have been considered too strict by administrators who bowed to community pressures. Coaches have been dismissed when they refused to "look the other way" after discovering instances of misbehavior by their athletes. Their principles and courage were no match for the school boards that served influential citizens.

Conversely, coaches are also fired for taking a permissive approach. They either have no rules or fail to enforce the ones they have.

As with many areas of coaching; laying the foundation of a code of conduct consists of measured calculation, clear-cut explanation, and resolute implementation.

An Illinois coach at a prominent suburban school created national news when he dismissed his entire varsity basketball team for staging an alcohol party in a hotel room during a Christmas tournament. The rules had been in place. The players had understood. The coach had no choice. Although backed by his administrators, he was so crushed by his players' disloyalty that he retired from teaching.

Do what you think is right—and have the sand to stand by it.

LIABILITY

Working with young people in a variety of physical activities creates vulnerability to litigation. Today's society embraces the lawsuit as a viable means of protection from malpractice—and a path to quick money. Professional educators carry the responsibility of rendering professional skills and services. Parents, school officials, and the community hold coaches accountable for preserving the well-being of their athletes during practices and games.

The arrival of certified trainers has been a godsend to ease the illness and injury burdens of high school coaching. Nevertheless, remain alert for new trends in health and safety. As an illustration, death or disability from heat illness during early season football drills can no longer be considered completely accidental. It is preventable in most cases, and coaches become derelict when they ignore such factors as temperature, humidity, clothing, and water consumption.

Football coaches must:

- identify and discontinue outdated and unsafe fundamental techniques, such as blocking and tackling with the helmet.
- eliminate outmoded attitudes about water breaks.
- conscientiously monitor weight training and flexibility activities for dangerous exercises.
- demand safe equipment.
- inspect playing areas and keep them hazard-free.
- avoid physical mismatches during contact sport drills.
- make vigilant supervision a habit.

LOSING

An athletic season is a period of knowledge and skill growth. Each practice and game become planks in the learning platform. Players learn from winning; they learn from losing. Healthy programs handle both with grace.

The inevitable result of athletic competition is that for each winner, there must be a loser. On the high school level, all but a few athletes will end their seasons and careers with losses. Take the time to guide athletes toward a healthy outlook regarding failure. Losing will not reduce their value as human beings.

Losing is inevitable. If values were based solely on winning, athletic participation would hardly be a worthwhile educational activity.

Counsel your players in managing the stigma of defeat. The goal of competition may be to play the perfect game, but we know total perfection to be impossible. The challenge comes from the pursuit—not the attainment—of perfection. By attacking the game with relentless effort, intelligence, skill, and spirit, your players will be champions regardless of the scoreboard tally.

At one school, our football teams left the game field each week by filing through an exit beneath the scoreboard. Players were instructed to: "Lift your heads as you pass under that board. Could you have changed those numbers with a better effort? Did you play as hard and as smart and as clean as you could have played? If you've done your best, keep your heads up and look to next week."

There must be winners and losers. Real losers give up or make excuses. We don't have to be perfect. The sin lies in not trying to be perfect. Losses come in the game of life, and life goes on. We grow by facing our adversities. Lessons from athletic participation come from losing as well as from winning.

As John Steinbeck wrote, "Somewhere in the world there is defeat for everyone. Some are destroyed by defeat, and some are made small and mean by victory. Greatness lives in one who triumphs equally over defeat and victory."

6

Teaching and Motivation

You may master your sport and develop a burning passion for your game, but a strong command of fundamentals, techniques, theories, and strategies does not guarantee coaching success.

Maury Waugh, veteran assistant football coach at Northwestern University and University of the Pacific, says, "I've seen many young people with absolutely brilliant athletic minds that just could never coach a lick. It's not what the coaches know, it's what the players know."

Coaching is the process of teaching individuals and teams of individuals to become better performers and better people. All great coaches have been strong teachers with abilities to explain and show "what...how...when...and why."

Vince Lombardi won five NFL Championships and two Super Bowls with the Green Bay Packers. He was a football genius and knew very little about basketball. Yet they remember him as a great basketball coach at St. Cecilia High School in Englewood, New Jersey. Lombardi also taught Latin and chemistry.

Bill McCartney led the University of Colorado football team to a national championship. He also led Divine Child High School in Dearborn, Michigan, to a *basketball* state championship. In essence, Lombardi and McCartney taught people perhaps more than they taught games.

X's and O's don't win games. Players win games. Lombardi said, "Coaches who can outline plays on a blackboard are a dime a dozen. The ones who win get inside their players and motivate."

Bob Frisk, a longtime dedicated and sincere champion of high school athletics, sends his weekly messages through the pages of Chicagoland's *Daily Herald*. He writes, "Coaching is teaching, and you cannot teach effectively for any length of time unless you can motivate your players to want to learn. It's very simple.

"The best game plan ever devised isn't worth the paper it's written on if the players aren't motivated to carry it out properly."

The subject of motivation rides a current wave of popularity. Successful college and professional coaches earn hefty fees for giving motivational speeches to business corporations. Bookstores carry volumes on motivational techniques. Coaches try to "fire up" their squads by:

- giving "Gipper" speeches.
- biting heads off frogs and birds.
- placing small figurines of rival team mascots in urinals.
- swallowing worms.
- smashing chalkboards, lockers, doors, windows, and wristwatches.
- manufacturing stories of a west coast team dressed as hayseeds when it arrived to play against a midwestern university.
- castrating bulls at football practice.

In 1993, a respected high school football coach wrecked an impressive 23-year career with one unfortunate error in judgment. Attempting to inflame his squad, he staged a phony fight between two students during a meeting before a crucial postseason game. One of the students—armed with a starter's pistol—fired at the coach as he pretended to break up the mock scuffle. Feigning a gunshot wound, the coach fell to the floor, bleeding tomato ketchup. Police responding to 911 calls (and school administrators responding to parent calls) failed to appreciate the coach's bizarre attempt to motivate. The act—not a stroke of genius at a time of community concern about guns in our schools—attracted world-wide media attention.

How this stunt correlates with motivating a group of high school athletes to play a better football game remains a mystery. The coach suffered at least two major losses following the incident. The big game—and his job.

Five months later, a Utah high school football coach (hardly an avid newspaper reader) fired a blank cartridge during geometry class. Working for a more lenient superintendent, this coach kept his job but was docked nine days' pay.

When players make sacrifices all season to become mentally and physically prepared for a big game, why would they need motivation to go out and play hard? In my view, becoming too excited poses a greater threat to effective performance. Some use motivational gimmicks most when they need them least.

Another high school football coach, obsessed with defeating his archrival, designed special practice jerseys and dedicated the season to beating the hated opponent. He won his game. But his team lost the other eight.

A.L. Trout had few peers as a motivational psychologist. He battled complacency by planting subtle challenges to nettle his players.

As an example, he once divided a basketball squad of average talent into two separate teams that shared playing time for the entire season. Trout dug his spurs in further when he named the teams "Buzz Boys" and "Molasses Men." He characterized the quicker five as a group that whizzed around the court with no apparent purpose. The "Molasses Men" were just plain slow. Besides the advantage of having a fresh team always on the floor, the coach enjoyed watching two highly motivated groups perform. Both teams played with fiery emotion as they competed for his approval—and more playing time.

We'll never know if a more orthodox approach would have improved that team's 26-6 record.

In other seasons, Mr. Trout occasionally shocked his boys when he selected a starting lineup at random. Each player from the full squad drew a number from a hat just before the game. Besides pumping up the morale of the less-skilled players, he inspired the original starters to play with extra vengeance.

Without slipping into negativity, Trout consistently used just the right amount of cynicism to goad his athletes. They couldn't wait to get on a field or court to "show him."

Read and listen to everything possible about motivation. Study your players' characteristics and personalities. And keep track of your own behavior.

Most of us would like to have Knute Rockne's gift for eloquent and emotional pep talks, but reality says we're all different. What works for some, works not for others. Players spot counterfeits quickly. John Prine would say, "You are what you are. And you ain't what you ain't." Develop *your* approach to motivation—one that's comfortable for *you.*

A reserved and deliberate coach could find "rah-rah" oratory and gimmicky stunts to be unnatural and awkward.

As a football coach, my personality called for a style that built and sustained a smoldering intensity by prodding players to practice hard and prepare thoroughly every day. We kept our practices and meetings purposeful and conducted them in a methodical manner.

Coaches led work in a relaxed climate during early-week preparations. As the week progressed, however, workouts turned dead serious and intensified with a growing sense of urgency.

A short talk at the close of the week's final practice closed all major communication. Along with reminders of game day details, we covered objectives and behavior expectations. To build an awareness of each team's role in the school's athletic tradition, we told war stories about players and teams from years past.

The goal of the talk? To establish a commitment to total effort toward intelligent and enthusiastic performance.

Game day dawned as one of deep resolution. Former players recall cereal dropping from spoons at their morning meal. Edgy uncertainty choked off all throughts of food.

We tried to keep the Friday school day as normal as possible. No special treatment.

Administrators could not understand or accept my aversion to pep assemblies. We needed no help with our enthusiasm or emotion. We had spent a week—maybe a year—doing that very thing. Showcases for cheerleaders, band members, and exhibitionist students and teachers were diversions rather than incentive devices.

Players endured bus rides to away games in absolute silence. They didn't talk. Coaches didn't talk. What kind of conversation could outweigh concentration on the job at hand?

Silence strangled the locker room. No music. No talk. No unnecessary movement. When an athlete sheepishly inched toward a bathroom, the clack of cleats on a concrete floor turned more heads than the rustle of a church bulletin in a silent congregation.

As game time approached, the coach stood before the

group and simply said, "It's a great night for football, Let's go play!"

Those words touched off a barrage of snapping chinstraps that exploded like an infantry firefight and signaled the start of the week's mission.

Although critics may question this motivational method for causing tightness and suffocating creativity, it worked for me in my situation. Coaching a different sport with more contests or working in an area that requires longer trips might be a different story.

I'm not so naive to believe that former players would unanimously endorse this coaching approach, but I believe our teams were ready to play on most Friday nights. It's gratifying to hear old players say they still get chills remembering those salvos of snapping chinstraps.

But an aggressive and restless leader could not endure the technique of building a measured atmosphere of quiet intensity. One with a natural knack for rubbing excitement off on others would be wrong to curb such enthusiasm while copying another coach's stoic approach. A coach with a more outward emotional makeup might do better with boom boxes, war paint, and pep rallies.

To be effective, operate within your own comfort level.

Coaches can easily underestimate the necessity of

sound motivational practices. Most have a deep love for their sport, or they wouldn't be coaching. As former successful athletes and fierce competitors, they assume all athletes have the same drive and compulsion to succeed. Athletes with different types of personalities and diversified attitudes, habits, and values make up teams. Constantly sell your convictions and expectations by incorporating a long-term plan of systematic motivation.

Study motivational methods to learn the importance of individual differences and the desirability of addressing each player's needs. Take caution, though, when coaching team sports. Unity and unselfish team play must not be compromised. The team always comes first. Players must understand that they surrender part of themselves for the good of the group. For this reason, some coaches do not put players' names on the backs of game jerseys.

William Warren, in his excellent book, *Coaching and Motivation* has sound advice:

> Surround yourself with players who love the sport; who respect you as a coach and believe that what you're trying to do for the team is best for them as well; who respect their teammates and feel a genuine need to perform well for their teammates sake as well as their own; who are willing to put in the necessary hours to

learn, and then to improve the skills associated with their sport; and who don't consider requiring them to play hard to be a kind of punishment. You can motivate those kinds of athletes.

The grind of a long season will test the best young people. Disappointing performance, limited playing time, peer and parental pressures, and a host of problems outside athletics can damage attitudes during the awkward years of adolescence.

Occasionally, you may be forced to cut a problem player from the team. Athletes who will not commit themselves to their coach or their teammates cannot be motivated or taught. Those convinced against their will are of the same opinion still.

Poor attitudes stifle individual development and threaten team growth by creating a hostile learning environment.

First year coaches in any situation can expect rocky roads as they establish their programs. Strong leaders bring problem athletes around—or cut them free for the common good.

My first head coaching experience, a basketball job in a small Illinois community, is an example.

Having a strong sense of "rights and wrongs, dos and

don'ts, and shalts and shalt nots," I did not hesitate to axe our starting center, a returning regular. Before the first game, the tall senior had brazenly skipped practice without permission. His choice to attend play rehearsal over basketball practice told me he should be an actor instead of an athlete.

By Christmas, the remaining four seniors had quit the squad. Shock waves surely rocked the small community of 4000, but I didn't hear them. Credit faith, tunnel vision, blind luck, and the staunch support of an incredible principal. Three sophomores and two juniors led that team to a .500 season. Testimony to the power of group spirit.

The following year, the little band of believers went 20-5 with a conference championship. And I went from a potential coaching zero to a living local hero. For a time.

Would I handle such a situation differently today? Scoldings? Stern warnings? Second chances? Maybe so. But as a history teacher, I learned early that appeasement did not work for Chamberlain at Munich. And it would not have worked for me at Aledo.

Some coaches have a different view. They will always be there for their kids. Their job is to help. They would never expel an athlete.

Professional coaches can trade problem players. How will you handle your undesirables? Run them off? Reform them? Or compromise your values and allow the passengers to fly the airplane?

Study human behavior to become a better teacher, motivator, and communicator. Read the books. Listen to respected teachers and coaches.

Kay McGuire, for instance, in *Winning Styles for Winning Coaches*, sums it up neatly:

> The successful person—in the athletic arena or the arena of life—can succeed only by making it possible for others to succeed.
>
> That's why we need to know what motivates others, what gratifies them, what hurts them, and what demoralizes them. We achieve that knowledge by learning their behavior styles. We turn that knowledge into a formula for victory by applying it in the light of the Golden Rule. We learn how others want to be treated. Then we try, to the best of our ability and circumstances, to treat them that way.

With proper preparation, you will make the right moves when faced with motivational decisions. Regardless of your chosen method of teaching and motivating, leave no doubt as to who leads the parade. Stand in command.

Win your athletes' trust and respect—and they will go to the wall for you.

7

Practice

After building a system of play, you must implement that system. Earlier, we established the importance of effective teaching and motivation. Practice is where it happens. Practices are teaching sessions. Games, meets, and matches are examinations.

The practice session forms the backbone of the athletic experience. It's the one daily occasion where all athletes and coaches come together. During this short time, coaches must:
- install a system of play.
- teach fundamentals.
- review previous games, meets, or matches.
- prepare for future games, meets, or matches.

- build team unity.
- teach moral values.
- indoctrinate sound health and hygiene practices.
- stress academics.
- instill strong work habits.
- develop dedication and sportsmanship.

ATTENDANCE

The first test of your teaching skills comes when you establish the sanctity of the practice session. Make players understand that practice is mandatory and cannot be missed without permission. Require that those unable to attend due to injury, illness, or other circumstances contact their coaches and discuss the nature of their situation. Conversations with athletes or parents can reveal the extent of injury or illness.

Nothing undermines team cohesiveness quicker than athletes who cut practice or show up late. This cannot be tolerated. You sabotage respect and credibility if you allow a double standard of athlete treatment to develop. Some coaches go by a "no practice—no play" rule. Some modify this to "no practice—no start." Many tolerate more. A few tolerate nothing.

Give clear and emphatic expectations for practice and game attendance. To prevent misunderstandings, make your position known to players, parents, and school administrators at the beginning of each season. Make practice rules especially specific for spring sports. Spring brings enough distractions to test the most patient coaches. They contend with bad weather, inadequate indoor practice facilities, ACT and SAT testing, spring vacations, Junior and Senior Proms, and graduation exercises.

Establish your policies. Be firm. Make practice a holy ritual. Make it sacred.

TEACHING

John Wooden, speaking at a University of Colorado clinic more than 40 years ago, divided the teaching process into four stages:

- Explanation.
- Demonstration.
- Correction.
- Repetition.

Use your best communication skills during explanation. Players can easily misunderstand what is being taught. Conduct the learning situation in a clear and concise manner, stressing the *why* as well as the *what* and the *how*. Keep your language simple, familiar, and explicit as you concentrate on one point at a time. Stress key points and repeat important information.

Most coaches like to keep their practices snappy and drill-filled. But during crucial teaching situations, you must take the time to reach your teaching goal. If meeting your objective means stopping drills for a lengthy explanation—or even leaving the practice area for a classroom atmosphere—so be it. Do what you have to do.

Coaches err when they assume their athletes understand every explanation. Check often to see that players are on the same page. Further teaching is fruitless if the athletes have not absorbed previous instruction.

Ask questions for feedback that verifies the extent of the listeners' grasp. But calling on knowledgeable or experienced volunteers may lead to the erroneous conclusion that the entire group gets the message. Question reluctant members of the group for a more accurate reading.

The players, after understanding the process, watch a demonstration performed live or viewed on film. Coaches and players should demonstrate only if they can perform with skill. A faulty effort may require re-teaching—a waste of precious time. Accumulate a backlog of film or videotape for demonstration.

A vital part of the learning process happens when athletes begin to perform the procedure. Analyze each performance and correct faulty execution promptly and enthusiastically. Be positive and evaluate *actions*—not people. Someone wise once said, "Practice makes perfect." Someone wiser said, "*Perfect* practice makes perfect." Avoid practicing how to be wrong.

Having fully understood what is to be learned, witnessed a demonstration, and correctly performed the task, athletes are now ready to repeat the performance. Repetition, the most effective method of athletic learning, enables players to respond to situations with spontaneity and confidence.

You hear and read about coaches who stress the importance of keeping all players involved in all practice activities. Standing around promotes laziness and weakens morale. This is sound advice for early practice days or the "tryout camp" stage. But once you find your players, things change. If you really want to win, give the repetitions to those who play the most. All players deserve equal respect and dignity, but they do not deserve equal repetitions.

Frank Leahy, the legendary coach at Notre Dame, said he would never use a play in a football game until his team had practiced it a thousand times.

Only geniuses—or the incredibly naive—dare scratch

new plays in the dirt on game day and run them without practice. Since most of us fit somewhere between brilliant and simple, let's stick with repetition.

ORGANIZATION AND PLANNING

We hear coaches praised for being well-organized. This is nothing more than knowing exactly what you want and exactly what you are doing. Adopt a plan—and work on it. Consider school philosophies, available facilities, and community traditions when you formulate practice procedures.

Make your practice routines compatible with the school atmosphere. Look at your school's position on the importance of athletics. Consider schoolday schedules, transportation policies, number of sports, and amount and types of practice areas. Be sensitive to other sports and activities. Your game may not be the only game in town.

Study the community and its traditions, habits, and customs. Coaches who work in the inner-city—where Reading, 'Riting, and 'Rithmatic have been replaced by Gangs, Graffiti, and Guns—operate much differently than those who work in affluent suburbs or in sleepy little towns where the population is the same as the speed limit.

Midnight Madness traditions—when fans pack the

high school gym at 12:01 a.m. each year to tip off the opening day of basketball practice—indicate substantial interest. When cheerleaders and the pep band pump up the crowd, school board members applaud from front row seats, the principal tosses up the first ball, and the superintendent makes sure that the Veterans Day break follows Midnight Madness, a basketball coach may sense a high level of practice freedom.

Four hour football practices in Pennsylvania steel towns may be routine, but scheduling a 30 minute workout on the opening day of deer season in some parts of Wisconsin could be foolhardy.

Careful planning, with deep concern for time management and realistic goals, is essential for successful practices. Establish a familiar practice routine for efficiency and time conservation. Limit explanations and directions to promote more spirited workouts.

Time is your foremost enemy. When addressing endless practice needs, rank those needs within the framework of time allotment.

Anticipation and preparation are the keys to prosperity. To quote an old Chinese proverb, "Dig the well before you are thirsty." Give your players the chance to handle any eventuality with success by addressing every phase of the game every day. Educators refer to this teaching concept as *distributive practice*, and it's not easy to incorporate. This method requires discipline, patience, hustle, concentration, and extra time. Use the difficulty of this daily crusade for perfection as a motivating device. Remind your team often that:

> We work on EVERY phase every day!
> We EXPECT good things to happen!
> We DESERVE good things to happen!
> We work LONGER!
> We work HARDER!
> We work SMARTER!
> We are BETTER PREPARED!

Use sound judgment when unexpected situations dictate a choice between reaching a practice goal—or staying within a time frame. Work with a time schedule, but don't become a slave to a manager's stopwatch and air horn. Don't smother flexibility for the sake of "being organized."

"Play 'em one at a time" is one of the oldest—and truest—coaching clichés. To escape the web of season expectations, concentrate on the game at hand. Go easy on long range goals. Take care of today's game, and let the season play out.

Consider abilities when making challenges and setting goals. Be practical and realistic in your expectations.

Take into account size, strength, and maturity differences when pairing off for contact drills. Besides the potential physical harm, mismatches may damage athletes' self-image.

As the season progresses, cut back. Vary your routine. Ease practice intensity with an occasional fun activity to elevate enthusiasm.

In football, for example, try field goal kicking contests. Or substitute offbeat relay races for wind sprints during conditioning.

An excellent fun activity for basketball is a "21" game using desperation shots. This drill improves passing and receiving skills, creates excitement, and generates extra running. And it delivers the bonus of accuracy improvement. As teams develop confidence, last-second attempts become more than hope shots.

One of my basketball players, interviewed after sinking a game-winning half-court basket at the buzzer, brought a smile to his coach's face. The newspaper account contained the player's answer to the question of how it felt to hit such a lucky shot. "Oh no, sir, that shot wasn't lucky. We practice desperation shots all the time—just like we practice every other part of the game."

Fight the urge to broaden your plans as you prepare

for your "big game." Players' anxieties may lead to tensions that inhibit their performance. They need no burden of added assignments. Many veteran coaches reduce work loads and trim strategic arsenals. The bigger the game, the simpler you get. Add surprise schemes only if they have been introduced and practiced previously.

While discussing the traditional NFL Thanksgiving Day game in Detroit for a *Sports Illustrated* article, Gary Danielson gave his view on the shortened work week. The former Lion quarterback says, "I've always thought that part of our success was that the coaches didn't have time to change. They had to stick with what we knew."

If you must prepare special schemes for future "big game" teams, devote a little time for that purpose each day throughout the season. Former Ohio State football players say that Woody Hayes spiced every practice with something to use against the season's final opponent—hated Michigan.

As a high school basketball coach, you may face the annual prospect of meeting an extremely strong and aggressive rival in postseason play. Make breaking their full-court press or solving their matchup zone a small part of your daily practice schedule. Don't wait for the week of your "must" game to prepare.

Many start and end each practice with a huddle. A

short message at the beginning previews practice objectives. Use a few words at the end to evaluate the session. Reinforce the athletes' self-esteem by making positive comments on their efforts. Encouragement motivates players to keep working to improve.

EVALUATING PERSONNEL

In team sports, a major practice objective is to evaluate players and select a starting lineup. This may not be as simple as it seems. At first glance, athletes who have the greatest talent would be the obvious choices. Merely rating players according to their athletic skills, though, may not be enough.

Milo Karhu, a former outstanding high school basketball coach in the Detroit area, confesses his biggest coaching mistake was assuming he should start the five best basketball players. He failed to realize, for example, that playing a big, rugged, dedicated kid with limited skills would make for a better team. He could neutralize more talented "big men" with his physical presence, hustle, attitude, and a willingness to defend and rebound.

"Instead," says Karhu, "as a 24 year-old head coach at a big suburban high school, I sat his physical presence on the end of my bench because of his limited offensive skills—and my limited experience."

Karhu feels he probably would have been more successful—and more kids would have enjoyed a better experience—had he cared more about things other than scoring baskets.

We are both benefactor and victim of our experiences. We can't make yesterday's decisions today. The best we can do is help others avoid our errors.

"If my son wanted to coach, this is the first lesson I'd teach him. It sounds crazy, but the best teams don't always play their best players."

As you search for the perfect personnel mixture to compose your team, be aware that some players perform better in practice than they do under game pressures. Others, with a history of less than impressive practice performance, have an innate flair for rising to a higher level when they face game night. These are the *gamers*. Recognize them and appreciate their value.

Al McGuire, the colorful ex-coach at Marquette University, likened himself to a symphony orchestra conductor who worked constantly to perfect the sound he wanted. Through motivation and communication, he used practice time for blending individual talents to generate maximum team performance. He devoted himself to managing people—and to coaching heads and hearts. He left most of the

X and O work to his assistants.

Athletes enjoy practicing what they do best. Only rare players work on their liabilities by themselves. Supervise their individual workouts and convince them that proper practice habits will turn weaknesses into strengths.

Live by the Cardinal Rule of Practice: You either get better or you get worse. You never stay the same!

Part II

Relationships

8

The Athletes

Success is more than juggling X's and O's, building powerful programs, and pushing young people to win—win—win. Although all jobs require winning (some demand much more than others), coaching is about people. It's about understanding community traditions, school philosophies, and neighborhood cultures.

As a high school coach, you face involvement with school administrators, fellow coaches and teachers, parents, booster groups, the community, media personnel, and college recruiters. The most neglected aspect of coaching, however, is the coach-player relationship. Always remember: Your chief responsibility goes to your players—your most precious resource.

CREDIBILITY

As you relate with your athletes, your most important asset is your credibility. You must inspire belief, respect, and trust. Trust—or the lack of it—comes when people see what you are and what you can do. Keep your actions consistent with your words.

You can't just talk. Live what you preach.

A sobering incident occurred during my career when parents of a former player gave me a paper written by their son as a requirement for a college writing course. The young man had fashioned a manuscript that described my sideline demeanor in astonishing detail; he had captured every mannerism.

Players note each act and expression. Be genuine. Be consistent. Maintain a balanced emotional level. Enjoy victory—but control the revelry. Denounce defeat—but deny depression. Players rely on your strength, stability, and fairness.

COMMUNICATION

Most coaches view efficient communication as speaking concisely and authoritatively, while their athletes listen attentively and obey promptly. They give lip service to the usual "my door is always open" invitation.

Stopping short of gutter talk, some coaches tighten their bonds with players by relating to them in a manner that teenage youngsters can buy. An occasional dip into high school vernacular can be effective.

Good communicators also listen well. Hear your players; but don't let them dictate your athletic philosophy, playing style, team rules, disciplinary policies, or practice schedules.

Two-way communication tightens relationships. Players become more willing to share feelings, concerns, and suggestions. Careful listening will not compromise your authority. Usually, coaches who complain about being the last to know have been too busy talking to hear.

SEPARATION

As you share the bonding experiences of a season's hardships and highlights, be wary of becoming too familiar. The small age gap between beginning coaches and their athletes may lead to excessive familiarity—which may lead to involvement in compromising situations. They are the players; you are the coach. Build a barrier between yourself and your athletes. You will develop leadership impact and respect if you establish and maintain a recognizable partition. Your personality, coupled with understanding the behavioral and personal characteristics of the team, will determine the height and width of the wall.

Some coaches forge close personal ties with their squads and still retain strong leadership roles. Others succeed by creating an atmosphere bordering on fear.

Arthur Trout combined a confident bearing with an authoritative edge. His intelligence, humor, compassion, and expertise as an educator inspired worship from his players and respect from his students. He was a sensitive husband, a loving father, and a statewide cult figure. He supported needy people and sheltered stray animals. Few players suffered the lash of his tongue. Yet most felt something beyond respect. Some felt fear.

His players sensed he cared for them. They also sensed he was prepared to replace them instantly with gym class students. He drew a line you dared not cross.

Although measuring a mere 5'6", his presence towered over others. John Lichtenfeldt, a no-nonsense local businessman with a hard-guy reputation, had been a member of a

Centralia state championship team. "Trout," said Lichtenfeldt, a fearless former college athlete who weighed 260 pounds, "is the only man in Illinois I'm afraid of."

Many coaches claim to seek only respect—not to be liked. What harm comes from enjoying both? Nearly all people want to be liked.

If you sense being disliked by your players, look for reasons. You may discover negative elements in your approach. By correcting relationship flaws and improving player-coach rapport, you may do a more productive all-around coaching job.

Don't court admiration or devotion. Get close enough to be a friend—yet stay distant enough to be a leader.

STRESS

Players can become *too* motivated. Trying extra hard and becoming too excited often cause anxieties. Stress may lead to mental or physical tightness that hinders maximum performance. Be alert for excessive tension—a growing menace to modern athletes. Coaches demand physical, mental, and emotional pursuit of perfection. Added pressures come from parents, the community, and fellow students. Players have concerns about media exposure—or lack of it. Add the heavy expectations athletes place on themselves, and some cannot cope with the tensions of competition. Documentation of mental depression and isolated suicides is scary. Be sensitive to changes in behavior patterns. Kids are human beings. They're not machines.

ACADEMICS

Added emphasis on academics, caused in part by increasingly stringent college entrance requirements, has led to greater involvement by coaches in athletes' classroom progress. Work with counselors to improve intelligent course selection, and monitor course work regularly. As you motivate your players to practice intensely, compete intelligently, and train faithfully, you must also insist on sound study habits and an appreciation for academics.

Above all—in some way—you must reach your players with perhaps the most striking message of their high school years. Life beyond school will not revolve around athletics. They must think beyond sports. Education is their key to a chance in life.

Athletes are your most valuable treasure. Take good care of them. Promote and sustain their development in mind, body, and spirit. Handle every player in a unique manner. Each one is different; each one is special. There is no magic formula. The good coaches mix harsh with gentle. Learn when to push—and when to back off. This separates the best from all the rest.

9

The Coaching Staff

THE HEAD COACH

As head coaches lead their athletes, they also lead their assistants. Advancements in the complexities of athletics have increased the importance of assistant coaches. Gone are those days when well-meaning sidekicks with scant athletic knowledge offered little more than companionship and comic relief. Head coaches can no longer handle every detail. They must delegate.

Most coaches hesitate to give up any of their responsibilities. Yet coaching in the modern world calls for training and trusting worthy assistants. Assign responsibilities to assistants and help them develop areas of expertise. Build your staff with as much pride as you build your team of players—and let your assistants share the glamour.

Football, with its large number of players and its natural breakdown of positions and skills, pioneered the efficient use of assistant coaches. Head coaches, faced with expanding intricacies and technological advancements in their game, needed knowledgeable, spirited, and loyal help.

Coaches of such individual sports as gymnastics and track and field have easily divided their sports into different events and appointed assistants accordingly.

The most recent change in the management of assistants is in basketball, where programs are isolating their offenses into guards, forwards, and centers. Some borrow football terminology and designate offensive and defensive coordinators.

The first step in building a strong coaching staff is to hire good people. Head coaches may have to accept being excluded from selecting assistants. In most cases, school administrators give top consideration to candidates' teaching credentials when employing new people. Incoming coaches must qualify for teaching available subjects. Once classroom requirements become satisfied, emphasis can shift to coaching duties.

Head coaches, if given screening and/or interviewing opportunities, should seek energetic, reliable, and loyal aspirants with strong interests in athletics and young people. Playing or coaching experience could be assets, but being a high quality individual comes first.

Many of the people-skills used in dealing with players apply to head coaches when they relate to their assistants. Assistant coaches, as well as athletes, often need motivation to become and remain dedicated role players on your team.

Assistants must be aware of your expectations. Make them clear. The indoctrination process gives an excellent opportunity to support your administrators. Remind your staff members that primary allegiance goes to their school. Teach first; coach second.

Your credibility means as much to your assistants as it does to your players. Shoot straight. Reliable and consistent leaders who maintain an emotionally balanced atmosphere earn respect.

Listen to your assistants, but avoid *coaching by committee.* Keep the final word, but take advantage of advice, opinions, and comments by your staff. Determine the extent of staff involvement in decision-making by judging the interests and abilities of your aides.

As you come to know your people, you will discover

different degrees of knowledge, ambition, and thirst for learning. Some will be content to merely ride along and collect paychecks. Know your people.

Be cautious with staff meetings. Time availability, classroom duties, and general athletic interest separate high school coaching from the collegiate and professional levels. Busy people—most with family obligations—form your staff. Few things sour attitudes faster than a meaningless coaches' meeting.

Keep in mind that your time is also valuable—too valuable to squander on democratic staff meetings that require discussions on every coaching decision.

Along with the obvious fieldwork support, good assistants provide excellent morale reinforcement. The strongest of head coaches experience periods of doubt, loneliness, and even fear. Those who coach long enough will see times when their best laid plans go south, their teams can't buy a victory, and their ears hear whispers around town. These are the times when loyal assistants come through. Treasure good help. Topnotch coaches have always known they cannot sail their ships alone.

While circumstances may limit your staff's commitment of time and involvement, strive to build and maintain camaraderie. Be generous with public praise for worthy assistants. Recognition and appreciation promote feelings of belonging and strengthen staff espirit.

All forms of leadership require a measure of detachment. Maintain your leadership role by drawing a line, however thin. Some assistants succumb to runaway ambition. Remember: It's your program.

Follow the Golden Rule of human relations. Allow your assistants the same freedom of expression and creativity that *you* wanted as an assistant. Unless their actions hurt your program, permit your staff to operate their areas of expertise with a generous degree of independence.

Staff members may wish to become head coaches— or move to a better assistant's job. Write letters and make telephone calls on their behalf. Support their efforts to advance. It's part of your obligation as a good head coach.

Even though your staff operates as a team and shares responsibilities, the head coach is liable for the program's direction. As the head coach, you must face the wolves when they howl. And they will howl. Count on it.

Others make suggestions. You make decisions.

THE ASSISTANT

Most coaches begin their careers as assistants. As an assistant coach, you owe allegiance to your school, to your head coach, and to building success at the varsity level. In handling lower level squads, never put winning games above teaching basic skills and building self-esteem. Your greatest gift to the program is a group of disciplined and fundamentally sound youngsters who love the game—and are eager to play again next season.

Carry a clear picture of your exact duties, freedoms, and restrictions. Accept your position as a subordinate. Be a team player and stay within your role. Clear all bright ideas with the head coach before you act. Shun personal publicity that could diminish the team concept. If you crave center stage and need the spotlight, do a favor for everybody. Try finding your own team—or try show business.

Respect your head coach as team spokesman (see Chapter 14 for more on media relations). Stay loyal when you relate with players, parents, fans, teaching colleagues, administrators, and the media. The competitive nature of athletics—along with coaching's countless strategic and personnel decisions—breeds wholesale criticism and second guessing. Steer clear of such trash.

10

The Classroom

All professional and most college coaches escape classroom responsibilities. High school coaches can expect heavy academic involvement.

Taylor Bell, veteran staff writer for the *Chicago Sun-Times* and the country's most vocal spokesman for prep sports, surveyed secondary school administrators and concluded that most look for four characteristics when hiring a coach. The typical principal seeks:

- an outstanding classroom teacher.
- a strong and fair disciplinarian.
- an effective motivator.
- a positive role model.

This may be idealistic in athletic hotbeds where winning games is a religion. Where defeating archrivals is more important than educating young people. But in most cases, coaches teach—and teach well.

Your driving interest may be narrowed to athletics, but you must recognize and accept your role as a teacher. If coaching is teaching, as has been so strongly stressed, you must be an effective teacher to be a competent coach. Your commitment to the education of young people—as well as your attitude toward administrators, fellow teachers, and students—will determine your success as a teacher.

In nearly every case, great coaches have been standout teachers. A.L.Trout's coaching skills made him an Illinois legend, but his classroom artistry earned near-reverence from his students. Today in Centralia, women above age 60 feel just as blessed to have been in his classroom as men feel proud to have played on his teams.

Lowell Spurgeon, the most brilliant football player ever developed by Trout, captained the University of Illinois team under Coach Bob Zuppke in 1937. He went on to become a prominent secondary school administrator. Spurgeon has been widely quoted as saying that Trout had not only been his greatest coach, but his finest teacher as well. "I had the privilege of being a 'student'—in every sense of the word—under the absolute best. Mr. Trout's influence on my life cannot be described. I will forever be grateful."

Dr. Alden Ray, Professor Emeritus at the University of Dayton and former Royal Society Research Fellow at the University of Birmingham in the United Kingdom, played football for Trout in 1948. Ray says, "Mr. Trout was the best classroom teacher I ever had—and I've had more than most."

Trout's civics and economics classes, always popular electives, filled up fast. Actor, entertainer, and gifted storyteller, he laced his lectures with humor and Bible quotations. His unique blend of philosophies and methods included no textbooks or homework.

The ultimate testimony to Trout's teaching skills came when fellow faculty members gave up their planning periods to sit in his classes.

His educational endeavors extended beyond the classroom. Former players recall how he turned game trips into learning experiences—from attendance at trials in southern Illinois courtrooms to tours of Chicago's Art Institute.

Dave Dorr, writing in the *St. Louis Post-Dispatch*, describes Bob Knight as a teacher with a philosophy of basketball borrowed from many. Dorr reports Robert Byrnes, an Indiana University professor, as saying that "Bobby is the greatest teacher I have ever seen."

Coaches stand out just as much within the school as

they do in the community, because athletics play such a major role in the school scene. Although most administrators become defensive about a program or coach growing too big, they understand the importance of competent athletic teams. When an athletic program becomes inept or chaotic, the public perceives the entire school to be in disarray.

Sports play a vital role in the development of a school's image. School spirit rises as athletic success rises. Administrators find their schools run more smoothly when their teams win.

Befriend and support your fellow teachers. Attend school functions and add to the spirit of faculty togetherness. Back your school at banquets and recognition ceremonies for other school activities. Send congratulatory notes to faculty and students who earn special honors.

Some faculty and administrators may resent your power and popularity. Others simply don't understand what you are trying to do. Write a newsletter to help you analyze actions, crystallize thoughts, and upgrade objectives. Send copies to faculty and administrators to improve understanding, tighten relationships, promote your program—and soften your toughest faultfinders.

Principals' egos equal those of coaches—and they dislike big surprises. As skippers of their scholastic ships, they deserve to know what you are doing and why you are doing it.

Be realistic when you judge your abilities and weigh your ambitions—and be patient. A promising young coach at a highly reputable school in a large midwestern district destroyed his career by waging a battle over classroom teaching procedures and philosophies. He defied his superiors, vowed to become a coaching success on the collegiate level, and resigned from the district with bitterness. He no longer coaches or teaches.

"I cried on the last day of school that year. God, how I loved coaching," he says. "But we got into a matter of principles—and I had to do what I knew was right. Even though other coaching things haven't worked out, I'd do the same thing again."

The hurt still fills his eyes.

Stand up for your program. But your game is not above other school functions. Coaches with a superiority complex isolate themselves from the school kinship group and forfeit that group's support. Athletic programs have enough natural enemies without antagonistic, avaricious, and self-centered coaches compounding the problem.

The coaching profession, complex and knotty at best, gets really rough when losses come more often than wins, or when unpopular decisions must be made. When storm clouds gather, buzzards circle, and the posse saddles up, you may appreciate a supportive school family.

Affection, admiration, and respect by students, teachers, and administrators have blunted many attempts by blustering community critics to steer besieged coaches toward the unemployment line.

Conscientious work in the classroom improves your reputation as a person with a sincere concern for teenagers and their educational growth. Students will detect your sensitivity to their needs and become enthusiastic followers.

During my career, I worked for ten principals. Each expected his coaches to be strong teachers. Just as you demand loyalty, dedication, and hard work from your players, your superiors deserve your best teaching efforts with an attitude of team spirit.

Memorable promises and observations by my first principal, Marvin Smith of Charleston, include the following:

- Even though you want only to coach, you *will* teach here.
- Give teaching a fair chance, and it will be more rewarding than coaching.
- Handle your own discipline.
- Teachers over six feet tall should never have a discipline problem.
- Make friends with the janitors. Custodians can help you more than any other school personnel.

My second principal, Bus Thoman of Aledo, made a permanent impression with his strong ideas about education. A retired navy commander, he greeted the faculty on the first day of classes each year with a five minute briefing (his version of a pre-school conference). He piped new teachers aboard and reminded the old hands that, "You know how much I've been opposed to the permissiveness of progressive education, and I haven't changed one bit. We run a tight ship here. The kids know it. The parents know it. The town knows it. And you know it. We're here only to teach and to learn. So damn the torpedoes...and let's get crackin'!"

On the final stop on my coaching trail, I outlasted seven principals and survived enough buzz words, catch phrases, precepts, platitudes, and cutting edge concepts to give Bus Thoman a permanent wince. I made it through SIS, TESA, OBE, self-actualization, collegial coaching, golden attitude awards, etc., etc., etc., only by following my father's advice: "If you sign on to work for a man...by god *work* for him."

Looking back at countless satisfying classroom moments makes a case for Marvin Smith's second observation. Great coaches are outstanding educators who just happen to work with athletes.

11

Officials

Television coverage of college and professional games encourages high school coaches to seek favorable calls by inciting crowds and intimidating officials. Many coaches, fans, media personalities—even school administrators—consider "working the refs" to be a positive coaching skill. Sad.

Competent coaches and able officials share the goal of orchestrating safe and well-played games. Effective officials conduct contests according to the rules, the spirit of the rules, and the "gray area" nuances—all with energetic spirit and no bias. Not an easy job.

At best, sporting society casts good-natured disapproval

toward referees. Crowds cheer playfully when an official suffers injury during competition. At worst, fans and coaches see referees as natural enemies who stand between their teams and victory.

At the same time, some officials consider coaches to be confrontational and threatening.

The old adage about walking a mile in another's moccasins applies to coaches and officials. A part of every coach's training should be a requirement to officiate at least one game. Officials should spend time preparing a team to play, and then watch the game from the bench. This will never happen, but it would bring swift advancement in positive coach-official relations. Each would approach the other in a new light. And neither would want the other's job.

A.L. Trout's brotherly relations with officials evolved, in part, from his early coaching experiences. During basketball's infancy in the early 1900s, coaches refereed their own games. Trout spoke often of the pressures of officiating those games, and insisted that players—and fans—respect officials.

In the 1930s and '40s, many assistant coaches supplemented meager incomes by officiating in nearby towns. As these young coaches moved on to head positions, they brought with them a high regard for officials.

Larry Peddy, longtime coach and 29 year veteran of officiating high school and college basketball games, recognizes the benefits of playing both roles. Peddy, who coached his baseball players to the Illinois state tournament and also officiated in the Illinois state basketball finals, found that becoming an official completely changed him as a baseball coach. After one season with the whistle, he just let go of being upset by the calling of balls, strikes, and close plays.

"As an official, I like to be around the *old-timers*—coaches who have gone through the process of what it is that gets you to a point of leaving officiating alone and just dealing with your kids," he says.

Young coaches start out wanting to be involved with the game. And the officiating. Good ones eventually settle into just teaching their game. Don't get so wrapped up with officials that you forget your kids.

When the old-timers have a legitimate question, they stand a good chance of being heard. And they stand a better chance if they question in such a way as to avoid showing up the official. Learn the difference between questioning and challenging or demanding.

Develop something more than making winning the only answer. It's possible to play as well as you can play—and still not win. You have to factor in the strength of your opponents. If you get the most out of what you have—but it's not good enough to beat anybody—you just have to be satisfied.

When it comes down to your needing a call and the other coach needing a call that finishes a game, be big enough to accept that call—even if it goes against you. Not all coaches can do that. The good ones can. They understand human fallibility and anticipate and accept isolated errors by officials—just as they must accept missed free throws, dropped touchdown passes, or throwing errors. They know it's their kids that win or lose. It's not those with the the stripes and whistles.

Your nerves catch fire on game night. You've invested years of collegiate instruction, clinic attendance, college campus visitations, extensive reading, film study, scouting, long practices, athlete counseling, and coping with parental and community pressures. Fans watch you succeed or fail. And the media documents it all. You view your games as crucial, because you understand the importance of adolescent development, the necessity of playing the game correctly, and the significance of success in the Win Column. You expect officials to share this urgency. You expect them to be on time, in good physical condition, neat in appearance, knowledgeable, and ready to give an honest and impartial effort.

Ideally, coaches and officials make every effort to master their respective trades. Both strive to become thorough professionals.

Good officials love their game and clean competition. They officiate as an avocation—a hobby—and receive minimal money. They attend meetings with their peers to discuss rules, mechanics, and unusual plays. They honor the game by directing action so that it is played the right way—with no concern for who wins and who loses. Good ones become tactful diplomats with a knack for game management. They learn to deal with players, coaches, and fans in a positive manner. Their reward for competence? Not glory or recognition. In fact, the nearer they get to perfection, the more invisible they become.

The 1995-96 NBA season saw increased assaults by players on each other and unprecedented physical attacks on referees. NBA referees worry about their own safety. The NBA brass worries about the league's image. My worry is about millions of impressionable youngsters who watch their idols attack authority figures. Is this the kind of respect we want our kids to show parents, teachers, and cops on the corner?

The fundamental cause of violence in sports is taunting—gestures and trash talk. During the heat of combat, with its game pressures and physical contact, abuse inflames tempers. Nobody—not even a small child—likes to be ridiculed or degraded. Such behavior has no place in athletics and can be stopped overnight.

The solution is simple. *It starts and ends with the coaches.* They can stop it. Or they can let it go. The professionals feel it's a big part of their game—and they pay the price. But in a sense, we all pay.

The National Federation of High School Associations now campaigns for better sportsmanship. It urges school officials to stress appropriate student behaviors and educate fans about proper decorum.

A large suburban high school near Chicago presents a trophy each year to the opposing school that exhibits the best sportsmanship.

The Illinois High School Association, conceding that schools cannot police themselves, enacted a sportsmanship by-law, effective July 1, 1995. Athletes or coaches ejected from a contest for unsportsmanlike conduct will receive a one game suspension. Those ousted more than once are suspended for the entire season.

You can eradicate most negative actions if you preach respect for officials and opponents, demand positive behaviors by players, and conduct yourself with class. Be conscious of your sideline manner. Lofty reputations, carefully built over many years, can be destroyed in an instant. Ohio State's Woody Hayes, by failing to collar his competitive intensity, damaged his image as a football coaching immortal with outbursts at officials. He finally shattered his reputation, his career, and perhaps his life in a sad few seconds of self-destruction.

Electricity generated by a capacity crowd, as it reacts to every turn with thunderous explosions of noise, makes big games exciting. We want to keep the thrill of an emotionally charged atmosphere. Coach with *your* personality. Animated coaches who are easily excited should be themselves. They deserve just as much respect as those who operate with a reserved approach—and they add color and flair to the games.

But challenging officials to gain an advantage is another story. When this happens, a side issue (playing the officials) replaces the central issue (playing the game). The coach changes from entertainer to inciter. Players react. Fans get into it. The primary focus is lost. And a spirited crowd turns ugly.

Question Bob Knight's basketball coaching tactics at Indiana University. But give him this: He tolerates no trash talk, taunts, or official-baiting from his players. And he's possibly the last coach in the country that can—and will—silence a vulgar home crowd with a dark glower and a wave of his hand. Yet, the next moment he disappoints and mystifies his admirers by raking an official.

Being the school disciplinarian—and with his name on the gymnasium—A.L. Trout kept a wholesome atmosphere in his building. More than once, when spectators grew nasty, he interrupted game action and lectured the rowdy crowd: "We don't do it this way in Centralia." And promised: "We can play this game without you people. Keep this up—and I'll clear the gym to prove it!"

School administrators should draw clear guidelines for crowd conduct and have the courage to enforce their expectations.

I never met a dishonest official, but my patience ran thinnest with those who failed to give their best efforts. Every official owes the players and coaches of both teams—and the game itself—a heads-up, hustling, and caring performance. My most volcanic confrontations occurred during those rare times when a referee with a history of working big games brought along a cavalier attitude that said he was above our level of competition.

Be aggressive with officials when they fall short in punctuality, appearance, competence, attitude, or effort.

Constructive criticism can be valuable as they progress in their careers. But send your messages behind closed doors. Both parties take heat more readily when it happens in private. Animated arguments always fuel a wild crowd's frenzy.

Unsound officials—as well as unsound coaches—should be educated, counseled, or eliminated. The game is too sacred to be profaned by dishonesty, incompetence, carelessness, or apathy.

Competition to win at any cost has spilled its venom into the decency of high school athletics and poisoned several aspects of interscholastic competition. Abuse of referees has contributed to an officiating crisis across the land. Older officials retire, and younger people find officiating to be unattractive. Low pay, great pressure, and limited advancement opportunities have always been detriments. Increased torment by coaches, players, and fans will only add to the problem. Beginners soon discover the long odds of one set of officials versus two sets of coaches, players, and fans. Many do not survive past the first two or three years.

Referees, umpires, and judges are as necessary to the game as are coaches, players, timers, and scorers. Encourage officials who are dedicated to the game and committed to the development of young people. State associations must reform their positions on qualifications, training, rating systems, and certification. They should promote higher pay scales and remove politics from assignment procedures.

The arrival of Title IX, and the growth of interscholastic sports for girls, has intensified the shortage.

Girls' sports suffer from inferior officiating. Weaker referees of boys' games become attracted to the smaller crowds, lesser pressures, and easier paychecks of girls' games. Stronger officials avoid working girls' sports, because they like the bigger crowds, better players, and higher pay.

A promising pool of officiating talent lies untapped. Women have demonstrated the ability to become legitimate first-rate officials at every level of competition. Heather McDaniel, a 5'5", 135-pound 24-year-old, officiates professional hockey games. McDaniel, is now under contract to the Central Hockey League.

Dee Kanter, handles a major college basketball schedule. Her work has been of such high caliber that she may become the first woman to referee in the NBA. Others predict the honor will go to Sandhi Ortiz-Del Valle, the first woman to officiate in a men's professional basketball game (USBL).

But too many ambitious young women with the desire and ability to become capable referees are discouraged by lower pay, discriminatory assignment practices, and minimal respect.

Officials who love the game and care about kids deserve gold medals for taking on the toughest job in any sporting competition. Good ones face extinction.

12

Parents

High school coaches shoulder heavier responsibilities of educating and handling parents than coaches who work on college and professional levels. The vast majority of parents show positive support as their children pass through the school scene and the athletic experience. Be aware, though, that parents can become problems. Some care too much. Some care not at all. Some just have no inkling.

Parents get involved early. Officials terminated a *fifth-grade instructional* basketball game when parents of opposing teams clashed. No physical blows were struck, but strong words, gestures, and threats by pitiful role models brought police to the scene.

A recent newspaper article described police breaking up a parking lot fight involving rival coaches and parents following a park district basketball game for eight and nine year olds.

Adolescence, with its turbulence and insecurity, often creates uncertainty and perplexity in parents as well as their children. Some with possessive natures become reluctant to "let go"—to give up their offspring to a controlling coach. Others relocate to other districts for a more advantageous athletic program. Some hold their children back at the elementary level to gain an edge in physical and social development. Many force youngsters to specialize in one sport before they have a chance to try other activities.

Along with a normal favoritism toward their offspring, some parents carry twisted views of their children's abilities. They expect heavy playing time and a college scholarship after graduation. Some pat the coach on the back with one hand while they whip up dissension with the other.

Some show a selfishness that demands the best for their children—often at the expense of others. Parental interference can retard an athlete's progress and undermine team unity.

Steve Tucker, writing in the *Chicago Sun-Times*, documented an extreme case of parental intervention when one of the best female high school basketball players in the United States became victimized by a parent-coach feud. Arguments concerning summer camps, access to the gymnasium, and game strategies led to missed practices, punctuality problems, suspensions, and benchings. When verbal quarrels turned into physical threats, school officials requested that off-duty police attend home games.

Further hostilities prompted assault charges against her father, as well as banishment from her games. She quit the team.

There were no winners. The father lost. The coach lost. The team lost. The school lost. The community lost. The game lost. And the player lost.

Horror stories of this type mandate a hard-line position on the place of parents in the program. Although positive relationships with all factions of your program are important, center your primary focus on your players. Concentrate on the athletes' attitudes and actions that bring maximum individual and team success.

At the beginning of each season, you and your team form a closed group to pursue perfection. Invite all outsiders—including parents—to support the mission and share the excitement that surrounds the games and activities. But leave no question regarding the place of outsiders.

Be pleasant and courteous to parents, but maintain an unmistakable distance. Deep friendships with parents can color personnel decisions.

Anticipate parental encroachment, and be quick to establish your stance. It's your program—built on your philosophy. Stand by it. Occasional parental displeasure is natural. Expect it. Be fair, but firm.

Peggy Scholten, one of a surprising number of men and women in Chicago's suburbs who coach boys' teams and girls' teams in the same sport, thinks coaches would have fewer problems with parents if they face them directly.

When each season begins, Scholten calls a short meeting with parents. In this session, she tells them—in very plain language—exactly what they can expect from her.

"Parents play a role in our cause, so I lay down the things I expect from them. They may not agree with any of it, but at least they understand my position."

The desire of people to be involved and to help with their children's activities has prompted the growth of parent clubs. Band parents support school music groups with no obvious problems. Parent clubs for athletes, however, sometimes beget trouble. The difference is the intensity level. In addition to normal interscholastic rivalry, the nature of sport leads to cutthroat contention for starting positions, playing time, postseason honors, college scholarships, etc.

Your approach to parent groups should be the same as to any interested parents. Avoid situations that demand or expect too much of your time or accountability. Be nice, but permit no invasion of your domain that would threaten team harmony.

Soften your approach to parents by occasionally showing your compassionate side. Sensitivity to others is not a sign of weakness; it's a sign of caring. When misfortune hits players' families, send condolences. Attend the wakes. When families celebrate, send congratulations. Never allow an athlete to leave a hospital following illness or injury without a visitation. Players' appreciation may be fleeting, but parents will always remember your kindness. Coaches from the old school routinely practiced such social graces, but younger ones may not have such protocol in mind today.

A tradition that develops parental rapport and support is the postseason banquet or program to honor the players. These ceremonies provide opportunities to reach parents. Use these occasions to familiarize them with your feelings. Tell them how important they are to their children and how most character traits—good and bad—start in the home. Promote your coaching philosophy. Educate them as to what sports should do for their children. Motivate parents to help their children build strong study habits. Encourage them to use school resources regarding recruiting, scholarships, and college entrance requirements.

Banquets allow you to thank athletes, cheerleaders, band members, parents, administrators, teachers, friends, and fans for backing your efforts to provide a positive athletic experience. And don't forget the pom pon squad, or you'll hear about it.

Be watchful for ideas that add unusual touches to these occasions. Try something different. Poetry, humorous stories, and sketches can be entertaining and add warmth to the festivities.

Players and parents love to hear their names, so personalize your remarks when possible. Give special notice to the seniors as they make their farewell appearances as squad members.

A midwestern football coach parlayed an idea of stringing together a few shopworn phrases and warmed-over jokes into a facetious tribute or "roast." It proved to be just corny enough to delight parents, players, and fans.

An enterprising young freshman wrestling coach used his workshop skills to range beyond the usual banquet awards presentations. He surprised each varsity wrestler with a homemade personalized plaque. The resulting flood of calls and letters to school officials reflected parental appreciation.

Each year, a northern Indiana football coach takes advantage of a staff member's technological talents to produce a documentary video to summarize the season and pay tribute to the players. The video records game action, homecoming highlights, pep rallies, shots of team members during practice sessions and road trips, musical themes, and creative narration. The presentation, a banquet tradition, spellbinds parents, players, and fans. Copies of the videos become priceless mementos.

Periodic newsletters filled with informative clips and inspirational notes promote positive feelings, and serve as one more way to reach players' homes.

Look into having a personal all-purpose card—maybe with a team logo—printed. The appreciation that comes from receiving holiday, birthday, congratulatory, sympathy, and thank you cards—especially with a personal note—is boundless.

You are limited only by your time, desire to communicate, and imagination. You may lack a creative touch, but you can enlist the help of friends, relatives, or townspeople gifted with words and ideas. Schools are rich with talented teachers who would contribute to your program.

Without the parents, we wouldn't have the kids.

Parents occasionally bring grief. They always have. Little has changed since 1792, when Mary Wollstonecraft noted, "Until society is very differently constituted, parents will insist on being obeyed, and will constantly endeavor to settle that power on a divine right which will not bear the investigation of reason."

Mary may have intended to define parents' attitudes toward their children, but she described perfectly what many parents expect from coaches.

13

The Community

Public relations skills may be more important to coaching success than won-lost records. Maintaining effective communications with athletes, students, administrators, faculty, parents, fellow coaches, and the media is essential for your program to prosper. But no segment of society will test your people-skills more sternly than will your community.

Rabid fans consider your position to be the most important job in town. They expect your teams to win. They care little about your views on scholastic progress or character development. They question your wisdom with every loss (or ugly win) and stand ready to help you coach. They have every answer—after the fact.

You may settle into a consolidated school situation in which you must juggle jealousies, suspicions, and inherent rivalries among several towns. And you can bet that citizens from each village keep a running score of which kids from where are playing.

In other settings with weaker athletic traditions, apathy may be the problem. You must spark interest and build enthusiasm. Poverty and the hopeless drug culture of inner-city neighborhoods will test any coach's ability to motivate athletic commitment. Some athletes' main goal is to make it to school and back home alive every day. Looking for a challenge? Try matching your academic, social, and moral standards with street values from a gang-infested ghetto.

All coaches deal with their adopted communities. Many feel immune to community involvement because of their special position. Some, in unique situations, may thrive as they violate rules of positive human relations. Yet a "public be damned" attitude can be fatal.

Study your community to better understand its culture. An appreciation of its history and traditions may smooth your road to coaching success. People see things differently near Houston's Astrodome, than they do along the Yukon—between Ketchikan and Nome.

The late Stuart Symington, U.S. Senator from

Missouri, learned to adjust to different environments as he moved about his constituency. In a single day, he could lead a meeting of big-city bureaucrats—and then enjoy a shirt-sleeved visit with a farmer as he leaned on an old top rail. He felt as comfortable in a faded flannel shirt at the counter of an Ozark truck stop as he did at a black-tie affair in Washington.

Two-faced? Hypocritical? No. The Senator had simply mastered the old "When in Rome" principle. Perfectly acceptable.

Communities usually have their booster clubs. Although fund-raising normally lies within the athletic director's jurisdiction, you may be expected to take part in money-making projects. Schools in some areas rely on these clubs to provide funds to subsidize athletic programs.

Some coaches feel comfortable with heavy involvement. They don't mind making the meetings, showing game film, and taking questions from the floor.

Others treat booster clubs like leper colonies.

Advice? Give booster clubs the same regard you would give any other part of the community. Be nice. Encourage them; they can be supportive. At the same time, be wary. They can boost—and they can burn.

The community watches with wide eyes. You work in the only profession that incorporates (and even advertises) weekly testing (with a pass or fail grade) in front of as many people as care to watch. The title of Coach elevates you to celebrity status, and your words and deeds glare under the community spotlight. Like it or not, you build your own image. Why not build a good one?

Many public relations authorities dislike referring to their field as *public relations.* Society tends to link that expression with blowing smoke, using mirrors, and manipulating people. Reputable professionals prefer to use the term *goodwill enhancement.* Their objective is to improve the image of a person, firm, or institution and to promote an atmosphere of warmth and support.

You don't need to hire a public relations consultant. Just practice a few principles of managing people. Don't wait for your *publics* —groups of people who share an interest in you and your program—to become aroused in crisis situations. Build a strong base of goodwill from the start.

Unlike most athletic games where defense usually wins, the public relations game features offense. Offense in public relations beats defensive PR every time—if it's a good offense.

My brother, Chuck Schnake, operates one of Tulsa's most powerful public relations firms. He advocates pushing pluses and minimizing minuses. "Some cynics—who are not happy unless they are miserable—define optimists as people who just don't have all the facts. We discourage pessimism. Folks don't want to hear about all the labor pains; they just want to see the baby."

A public relations principle: When dispensing information to any group, release bad news all at once to reduce lingering negativity. Let the healing begin.

Good news, on the other hand, should be dished out a little at a time to prolong a positive climate.

Chuck refers to the fundamental workings of a job as being trench work. Some people become obsessed with digging their trenches. Heads down. Jaws clenched. Sweat streaming.

Coaches—fixated with fundamentals, strategies, or X's and O's—cloud their visions of overall responsibilities. Unfortunately, most go no further than trench work—trying to add another victory to the win column.

Cultivate a better working relationship with your many publics by periodically climbing out from your trench for a view from the hilltop.

Take in the fresh air, and look down at the grand scheme of things with dancing eyes and a knowing grin. Rise above concerns about petty dissent from a few opinionated radicals.

Your sense of calling must tell you there is more to coaching than plotting (or plodding) to win ball games, matches, or meets.

Coaches have their own styles of operating with the public. They range from complete non-recognition to aggressive interaction. Personality makeup has a lot to do with how people interact with other people.

Few coaches have maneuvered crusty and ill-tempered fans with more color, conviction, and courage than Coach Trout.

Outstanding athletic success and a high tide of community enthusiasm combined to breed a thorny batch of Downtown Coaches. Tagging the small gang of malcontents as *Termites*—tiny individuals that fed on the "wooden heads" of his athletes—Trout recognized this group for what it was. He dealt with it head-on and never gave an inch.

Trout vs. the Termites turned into a series of encounters that often rivaled the games themselves in popularity. He treated his run-ins with the Termites as a game, and he played it with gusto.

The son of a Christian minister, Mr. Trout freely quoted scripture as he lectured his players on the practice field and his students in the classroom. During team meetings, he addressed the Termite Problem by cautioning his players to

"Beware of false prophets, which come to you dressed as harmless sheep, but inwardly they are ravening wolves."

He supplied his teams with identities, locations, and evil motives of Termite Club members—a hardware store owner, barber shop operator, local attorney, etc.

He commissioned an artistically talented member of his basketball squad to create a group portrait of the five starting players being ravaged by insects labeled with names of the town's most prominent Termites. Then, he displayed the caricature in the gymnasium's trophy case to make his point.

One year, the old coach silenced downtown complaints about his basketball team wearing soiled uniforms. Instead of laundering them more often, he replaced the traditional cardinal and white outfits with an all-black set. Then he winked as he told a reporter, "Now let's just see if they can tell if they're dirty or not!"

The Termites questioned Trout's promotion of a talented freshman basketball player to the starting lineup, and that led to another stir. "Not ready!" "Too young!" "Green!" and "Needs seasoning!" came the cries. Before an overflow home crowd, Coach Trout decorated the youngster with an assortment of vegetables and spices, sprinkled him with salt and pepper, picked up the microphone at the scorer's table—

and proclaimed the boy to be duly seasoned. Case closed.

Emulating Mr. Trout's aggressive stance with the community may not be your answer to handling rabid fans. A unique bundle of whimsical nonconformity, Trout shattered standard coaching rituals in nearly everything he did. Let your personality determine your course.

When you're on top, everybody's with you. When you sink, you sink alone. The nature of coaching calls for inevitable second-guessing. You will be analyzed, criticized, and stigmatized. Face your critics with the confidence that comes from doing all the right things for all the right reasons.

Buffalo Bills coach Marv Levy says, "Some things are politically correct. Some things are popular. Some things are right. What is important is that you do what is right."

As Abraham Lincoln once put it, "I do the very best I know how—the very best I can—and I mean to keep doing so until the end. If the end brings me out all right, what is said against me won't amount to anything. If the end brings me out wrong, ten angels swearing I was right would make no difference."

14

College Recruiters

How responsible should you be for getting your athletes into college?

Some feel no commitment to their players beyond the final game of their last season. Teachers of history, English, mathematics, or science rarely feel an obligation to direct students' lives beyond high school graduation. Some coaches share that attitude and resent the distractions and time demands of the recruiting process. Such coaches discourage telephone calls and visitations. They stockpile players' letters and questionnaires until season's end.

At the opposite extreme, some control the recruiting process with a death grip by screening colleges and steering players to schools of the coaches' choice. They base their rationale on the assumption that players and parents lack the expertise to understand and manage such a procedure. In isolated cases, rumors have coaches taking money in return for arranged meetings, telephone calls, campus visits, and college selection.

Most coaches deal with athlete recruitment somewhere between the two extremes. Basically, athletes and their families should navigate their own paths beyond high school. They must live with their choices. The coach's role should center on educating and counseling families regarding the ground rules of recruitment—and how to cooperate with college coaches.

Ideally, coaches and family members develop a working arrangement to formulate guidelines, goals, and strategies. The first barrier to a cooperative effort is a mutual agreement about athletic ability. Parents (notoriously poor evaluators) often unrealistically assess their children's talent. Consider obtaining opposing coaches' opinions. Talent scouting services also make judgments by studying videotapes or film.

Coaches can:

- educate players and parents about college entrance requirements.

- return inquiry forms to colleges.
- forward letters and questionnaires to players.
- send videotapes and film to colleges.
- contact college coaches.
- make themselves and their athletes available to recruiters.
- have transcripts and highlight film available when college coaches visit.
- assemble brochures with vital information and positive comments.

Keep your marketing efforts objective and honest. Some coaches push their favorites or promote undeserving children of influential parents. Lies about 40 yard dash times, weight lifting accomplishments, or vertical jump measurements destroy credibility with college recruiters. Cooperation and honesty improve future recruiting efforts. Establish a positive reputation in the college coaches' network. Solid relationships with recruiters afford bonus opportunities to keep current with coaching's latest trends and innovations.

The process of placing athletes into colleges—especially when it involves blue-chippers—can turn your season into a circus. Protect your players, your team, and yourself by imposing strict rules. Your athletes' home lives and study climates must not be damaged by avalanches of phone calls. Don't allow recruiting pressures to interfere with team practices or game preparation. Help players win scholarships, but remember your primary responsibility. The team comes first.

Parents, new to the hectic and often confusing world of recruiting, need help. Offer them the following tips:

- Obtain and study a free copy of the NCAA handbook of recruiting rules.
- Be realistic about athletes' abilities.
- Determine what athletes want; generally, they know where they can play.
- Be in control—but be willing to use the high school coach as a resource.
- Consider using commercial videotapes that explain the fundamentals of the recruiting game.
- Grasp the idea that Division I programs emphasize winning games and making money.
- Realize that recruiting is an enormously competitive business—a cutthroat game with high stakes.
- Shift emphasis from making the pros to getting a solid education.
- Ask about graduation rates, academic support services, academic advisers, and progress monitors.
- Consider the odds (greater than 6,000 to 1) of a high school football player reaching the NFL.
- Consider the odds (greater than 10,000 to 1) of a high school basketball player reaching the NBA.
- Know that recruiting begins during the junior year.
- Recognize that letters from colleges indicate awareness—not recruitment. Telephone calls are the real signs of seriousness.
- Understand that college recruiters seek size, speed,

and skill—plus potential. Clippings, postseason honors, and statistics rarely impress them.

The latest development in the recruiting wars involves *street agents*. Outsiders befriend young—often grammar school aged—"can't miss" prospects (predominantly basketball players in urban areas), form a strong bond, and sell them to big-time college programs. A national scandal will surely erupt from this practice. Parents and high school coaches must stay wary of self-serving outsiders who wedge into parent-child and coach-athlete relationships.

Ideally, a panel of counselors, administrators, parents, coaches, and athletes would make sound decisions based on all components of collegiate life.

Each year, for mysterious reasons, athletes with qualifications equal to or better than those who are awarded Division I scholarships receive no offers. Recruiters make mistakes. Be prepared to deal with disappointed kids and parents whose telephones fail to ring. More than a million boys and girls play high school basketball each year. They compete for 30,000 college basketball scholarships. Less than three in each 100 will play beyond high school, and the majority of those will go to Division II and III schools.

College coaches' inaccurate evaluations, increased NCAA recruiting limitations, and reduced scholarships cause worthy players to be overlooked. They may need outside marketing help.

Recruiting analysts provide evaluation and placement services for colleges and for high school athletes. Investigate their legitimacy. Some use their services as fronts for operating lucrative summer camps—while they make unkept promises and give overblown talent evaluations.

Summer camps began as places where players had fun and refined skills. Many camps took advantage of the growth of high school sports and the insanity of recruiting competitiveness. They changed from being instructional to being exploitive. Familiarize yourself with a camp's motives before you encourage a player to attend.

Many talent scouts run legitimate (though often expensive) services that place deserving youngsters with colleges and universities. By making film and videotape—along with comprehensive player profiles—available to college coaches, these agencies help both sides involved in the recruiting game.

Today's computer age allows services to connect high school athletes with collegiate programs via the Internet. Such companies also benefit smaller colleges with limited resources in their search for athletes.

Help your players advance to college. Offer information, support, and encouragement—but place the ultimate decision in the hands of the athletes and their parents.

15

The Media

Coaches wage constant war with the clock as they go about their coaching chores. Who needs media requests for photographs, rosters, schedules, interviews, and other seemingly endless impositions? Be patient with the press.

Negative public sentiment has driven companies out of business. And it can drive you out of coaching.

Newspapers, radio, and television dramatically affect the lives of professional and college coaches. Prep sports may receive relatively light coverage in the metropolitan press, but smaller community newspapers often give huge publicity to their high school heroes. Some towns, for example, shower their high school football programs with far more publicity and community support than they give their local universities. West Texas high school quarterback controversies can be more heated than any in the NFL.

You may receive limited coverage in your area, but the press is still important. Regardless of the quantity and scope of reportage, be grateful for quality. Be thankful when newspaper and radio people respect the innocence of high school sports and withhold critical commentary.

The mass communications industry has a powerful hold over people and their attitudes. The public tends to treat the written word as gospel—"That must be true; I read it in the paper." Try to understand the media. Cooperate with those who work in all forms of communication, and respect their ability to influence readers and listeners. They may even learn to like you.

Is there some stigma attached to being likable? What is lost by being a pleasant human being?

Leo Durocher's enduring statement that "nice guys finish last" has confused many young coaches—and older ones too. Durocher, were he alive today, just might admit that he meant "weak" when he said "nice."

Take advantage of one of human nature's laws: It's easier to be easy on friendly people. Coaches who wage war with the media invariably lose those wars—unless their teams win often and win big.

Anger flares when the press misquotes a coach, or when a coach senses a slanted or distorted story. Handle these situations in much the same manner as you manage coach-athlete, coach-administrator, or head coach-assistant coach disputes. Face-to-face meetings behind closed doors usually ward off festering ill will. Those who truly want harmony will be able to reach harmony.

Be patient with inexperienced or incompetent writers. Better to educate the press than to clash with it.

A friendly press often helps coaches define their programs for their publics. Coaching is about wins and losses. But it's also about teaching values and preparing youngsters for life. Coaches seldom communicate this side of coaching to their publics. They should. Take every opportunity to send reminders that many yardsticks measure coaching proficiency—not just one.

Occasionally, the press serves as a platform for public debate and offers coaches additional opportunities to air their beliefs and defend their philosophies. Normally, avoid confrontations over petty problems with the community. Every town has its critics with their usual complaints. Sometimes, though, you may be driven to answer attacks.

In the early days of World War II, A.L. Trout marched

to battle—with a pen as his weapon—to defend his views. In an open letter, one who signed himself as "Sports Lover" attacked Trout in the *Centralia Sentinel*. He charged the coach with emphasizing victories and glorifying a few first team members while denying the bulk of the students the advantages of physical training.

Coach Trout countered:

> Boys who fail to make our high school teams are not denied an opportunity to develop physical fitness. Neither are the girls. Our school board employs full-time physical education instructors who attend to that...all day long.
>
> To your charge that we try to have teams that win, and win fairly, I plead guilty. This wish to be a winner, though, is not considered to be an evil thing in other sections of this fair land. People try to win at checkers and bridge and poker and croquet and in contests for Queen of This and Queen of That. Political parties try to win elections. We—all of us I hope—are seriously and desperately determined to win from the Germans and the Japanese.
>
> And through all recorded history, winners have been acclaimed, and crowns have been awarded—to use the scriptural phraseology. Do you wish to decorate with a medal for valor, the man who ran away, instead of the

one who led the charge? Or, are you against rewards of winning for anyone and anything? What's wrong with winning, anyway?

When you discuss opponents' abilities in the news media, heed Bear Bryant's advice. Always say nice things—even if you have to stretch the truth. Why arouse opponents with braggadocio or inflammatory remarks?

Bryant may have manipulated the press, but most coaches who stand accused of so-called "poor mouthing" feel bona fide concern over their opponents' capabilities. From "Stagg Fears Purdue" to "Leahy Predicts No Notre Dame First Downs" to "Holtz Dreads Navy," headlines have chronicled the anxieties of veteran campaigners. They have witnessed enough upsets to know how easily things can go wrong.

Those who court the media or "chase the ink" can acquire reputations as negative as those who shun reporters or those who greet the press with hostility. Being center stage, you draw more than ordinary media coverage. Be careful of self-glorification. Cultivate a viewpoint that the media spotlights you and your players for what you are doing—not for who you are. Advise your players—and remind yourself—that you cannot keep your eyes on the prize, if they're too busy reading press clippings.

The head coach acts as team spokesman. Though they mean well, assistants may make inaccurate or improper statements during press interviews. Head coaches design, build, and maintain their programs. They are accountable. They understand the image they wish to project. To maintain a consistent party line of policies and principles, the head coach talks. Assistant coaches listen.

Some coaches muzzle their players to prevent unwanted comments from appearing in print. This practice damages a positive relationship with reporters. Many editors expect their writers' stories to include players' quotes.

Properly handled, media coverage can be a valuable tool for educating youngsters and raising team morale. Instruct your players in the fundamentals of saying the right things when meeting the press. Teach them to be modest, give respect to opponents, and give credit to teammates. The star running back endears himself to his linemen when he publicly praises the individuals who block for him. The no-hit pitcher tightens team unity by crediting the catcher who called the game—and the fielders who made the plays.

Reporters have their jobs to do, and they deserve more than a "no comment." They affect your image, so boost your program—and yourself. Make a friend of your local scribe.

Part III

Sundries

16

Boys and Girls Together

The most dramatic development to affect high school coaches began in 1972 with the enactment of Title IX. This provision mandated that federally funded schools produce and promote equal athletic opportunities for both sexes. Title IX promised girls' sports a balance in the areas of monies spent, practice and game facilities, practice times, and publicity. Most schools formulated policies to equate the interests and abilities of all students.

Although falling short of perfection—with schools in some areas paying little or no heed—the implementation of Title IX has created a significant surge in girls' programs. Before 1972, many state associations banned girls from playing interscholastic sports. Even after Title IX's arrival, several states continued segregation by legislating by-laws to assure that:

- boys play on boys' teams.
- girls play on girls' teams.
- men coach boys.
- women coach girls.
- men officiate boys' games.
- women officiate girls' games.

Since 1972, female participation in interscholastic sports has experienced immense growth. The National Federation of State High School Associations reports that 2,240,461 girls played high school sports during the 1994-95 school year—an increase of 115,706 over 1992-94. During the same time period, however, the number of male players decreased slightly.

Given the competitive nature of sports, athletes of both sexes soon challenged coaches, school officials, and the courts to cross gender lines in interscholastic athletics. Girls want to play football and wrestle. Boys want to join bowling and field hockey teams.

Ila Borders, along with her coach, braved profane and obscene insults by opposing players and fans as she became the first woman to pitch on a men's collegiate baseball team at Southern California College.

Pamela Davis fared much better on June 4, 1996, when she pitched for Class AA Jacksonville, an affiliate of the Detroit Tigers, in an exhibition game. The 21-year-old right-hander earned a victory—and became the first woman to play for a major-league farm club. She enjoyed a standing ovation from the fans (complete with curtain call) and high-fives from her teammates.

Stay tuned.

While some treat crossing over as a sport in itself and revel in the attention created by breaking new ground, they usually defend their action by claiming their right to participate in a sport not offered to their own gender.

News items that sprout from such activities have slipped from sensational to routine. The idea of girls playing football has gone from an unthinkable concept to stark reality. Despite doctors' warnings that female physiques are inadequate for tackle football, girls continue to challenge the system. Records reveal that 334 girls competed for their high school gridiron teams in the U.S. in 1993.

An Illinois high school freshman female baseball pitcher was denied the opportunity to join the boys' baseball team, although her skills in pitching and hitting were proven through years of youth league competition. Reason? The school fields a girls' softball team. Fact? Overhand pitching makes baseball a different game. The Illinois High School Association has since reversed its ruling.

Few Americans realize that in the Arctic Circle's frozen bush, tiny villages of basketball-crazy Alaskans think nothing of mixing boys with girls in their high school lineups. With enrollments ranging from between five and 50 in the Class 1A division, they have small choice...and suffer little.

Yet most girls achieve greater enjoyment and success by staying on teams of their own gender, because of disadvantages in size and strength.

Advocates of coed sports point to increased mutual respect, shared learning experiences, and the development of important life skills as benefits. They place greater emphasis on high school athletics as learning enrichment activities—rather than games to amuse the community and to train future college athletes.

Others, however, predict that the invasion of boys into girls' activities will damage the progression of girls' sports.

In the early years of Title IX, women dominated the coaching of girls' teams. Typically, they stressed the educational and social aspects of sports—and shied away from the growing pressures moving in from the boys' games. As demands to win, to entertain large crowds, and to produce college scholarships escalated, women coaches became competitive technicians, tacticians, and motivators—or they faded from the coaching scene.

Proliferation of women coaches suffered additional setbacks when jobs failed to open due to an over-supply of teachers for declining enrollments.

Today, ladies are returning to the coaching ranks. Female athletes who learned to compete under the heavy pressures have grown into women who want to coach. They are willing and eager to take on challenges from parents and fans—and to answer scholarship expectations.

As more women move into administrative power positions, they threaten gender tranquillity. Men who aspire to coach women's sports shout, "Discrimination!" Qualified men who suspect some schools use quota systems and unwritten hiring policies to promote women in coaching claim they have been denied equal access to openings.

A Division I women's head basketball coach lodged a multi-million dollar lawsuit against her university and its athletic director. She claimed sex discrimination because she is paid less than the men's coach.

Another women's basketball coach filed suit against her university and three athletic department officials. She alleged violation of state and federal laws when she was fired for speaking out in favor of gender equity.

Universities make headlines by dropping mens' sports in attempts to reach gender balance. Charges of reverse discrimination echoed through the University of Illinois as it jettisoned its men's swimming team—and kept the women's squad.

College football coaches battle advocates of women's sports who propose cutting back football scholarships. They accuse "militant women" of trying to destroy football and tear down men's programs, rather than making efforts to build up their own.

When rumors and charges of gender inequality produce incendiary atmospheres on collegiate scenes, can conflicts in high school situations be far behind? A woman coach recently filed suit against a prominent midwest suburban high school district. She sought an appropriate facility on the campus for her girls' softball team and deemed daily busing to a distant field—while boys' baseball squads played and practiced on campus diamonds—to be an inequity. She won.

Should men coach girls? Or women coach boys?

Dorothy Gaters coaches the girls' basketball team at Chicago Marshall and is widely acclaimed to be the nation's best. Few can argue when they consider her 571 victories and six state titles. The only girl's coach in the nation with a higher winning percentage retired in 1970. Coach Gaters has been quoted as saying that women should coach women, men should coach men, and athletes relate better to coaches of the same sex.

Some girls say they prefer playing for men; males motivate better, work harder, discipline stronger and demand more. These girls did not play for Dorothy Gaters.

Marcia Krysh, the highly successful and respected girls' basketball coach who led Elk Grove High School to the 1981 Illinois state title, believes that who coaches whom doesn't matter.

Some women seem to understand—and have a feel for certain sports—like volleyball. Boys seem to sense that, and in a lot of cases the ladies do a better job of coaching boys than men do. They are earning solid reputations with their outstanding boys' teams. Of course, winning helps and keeping their teams near the top in the state rankings gains respect from their players, their communities, and from their rival male coaches.

"I really don't think it's a boy-girl thing," says Krysh. "Aside from concern about locker room situations, it still boils down to individuals—male or female—who know their game and who understand and care about kids."

Peggy Scholten, who has handled girls' volleyball for

19 years and has coached the boys for seven seasons at the same school, sees no reason for men not coaching girls or for women not coaching boys. Any person with an understanding of the game, teaching and motivating abilities, sensitivity to adolescents, communication skills, good work habits, and confidence should be able to coach boys *or* girls.

"I do see differences," Scholten says, "beyond the obvious. Boys seem to have extreme innate competitiveness. They show great focus, play aggressively, and tend to specialize.

"Girls require greater motivation. And generally lean toward a social approach to their game. It's important to them to 'belong' in the school scene, so they like to play other sports and participate in other activities."

Athletes, parents, and school officials endorse her energetic and hard-nosed approach. "You earn respect," she says, "by the job you do—whether you work with boys or girls."

When Elk Grove High School began addressing Title IX requirements by adding girls' sports, Ken Grams reluctantly volunteered to add girls' softball to his coaching duties. A popular and effective boys' head basketball coach in the Chicago suburb, Grams soon dropped his basketball job and has earned recognition as one of the top softball coaches in

Illinois.

"The first appealing thing about coaching girls," he says, "was seeing immediate results. Having had little or no previous serious instruction, they responded with a real eagerness and improved dramatically."

Grams notes another difference. Girls have less ambition to play beyond high school. They're less wrapped up in college scholarships or professional careers. "By and large," he continues, "most girls are in it for fun and sociability."

He works as hard with the girls as he did with the boys—the clinics, the off-season work, and all the preparation details—and believes they try as hard as the boys and want to win just as much. Girls, though, seem to have a "life goes on" way of thinking. Their jubilation over a victory lasts about three minutes; their depression over defeat lasts about the same. Maybe all high school sports ought to be that way.

Young women are finding that more favorable teacher/job ratios are leading to increased coaching opportunities. They will also discover that while Title IX has forced schools to recognize the importance of girls' sports, inequalities continue to exist in many districts.

Coach Krysh, who doubles as the Elk Grove girls' sports coordinator, says, "Although our school has been extremely cooperative with our girls' programs, we still struggle. For instance, janitors will not hesitate to barge into one of our practices to attend to some repair job. These same people wouldn't even think of interrupting a boys' practice."

Boys' basketball teams automatically expect to film or videotape their games. Girls' coaches may have to press full-court to get equal treatment.

Beginning basketball coaches may find that paid scorers accompany boys' teams—but not girls' teams—on the road.

"These are just little things," she says, "but young coaches should be prepared to stand up for their share of prime time practice, access to acceptable playing and practice facilities, and favorable budgets. And be aware that in many ways, it's still pretty much a 'man's world' out there."

Man's world? Illinois' top girls' basketball team recently hosted the country's No.1 ranked squad from Ohio. Played before a packed gymnasium and a nation's eyes, the game showcased great players, outstanding competition, and the conspicuous absence of cheerleaders for the Illinois team. The school assigned no cheerleading squad to girls' basketball. The pep squad spent the evening rooting for the boys' team (with its losing record) at a road game.

Gender-balance issues must be faced; girls' athletics will remain a force in high school sports. Title IX is the law of the land; it's not going to change.

Harmonious coexistence will happen only when:

- girls' coaches push for respect and equality with diplomatic patience.
- boys' coaches develop and maintain cooperative attitudes.
- school administrators recognize their responsibilities toward gender justice.

Until then, equality issues continue to smolder.

17

Getting the Job

The preceding material details the importance of a solid high school athletic program and offers suggestions about how to build one. It shares insights into handling vital relationships with coaching's many publics. And it encourages high school coaches to go beyond X's and O's or Wins and Losses. But it does not tell how to get a job.

Coaches new to the profession—and lacking the contacts developed by those already in the field—often have trouble entering the job market. In addition to using college placement services, aspirants may mail inquiries to athletic directors of area schools. Check newspapers. Larger suburban sports sections now list high school coaching vacancies.

Before plunging into a first coaching venture or advancing to a more challenging position, you must clear the hurdles of application letters and job interviews. With our history of laymen serving as decision-making public school board members, high school coaches field a wide assortment of strange questions during unusual interviews—particularly in smaller school systems. Interviews during my job-seeking days included conversations with a colorful cast of characters.

I once faced a board member who held court high atop his John Deere in an 80 acre cornfield. With hat in hand, I marveled at this prime example of how power positioning can intimidate. Lost the job. Should have worn bib overalls and a seed cap.

A principal once squeezed my interview into his busy schedule by mixing questions with practice swings on a fairway of the local golf course. Lost the job. Should have offered to caddie.

Another principal conducted our preliminary interview in his '42 Chevy coupe as we sped along dusty backroads to meet an eccentric board member. The wealthy farmer delighted in his extensive vocabulary and enjoyed stumping candidates with pompous questions. Lost the job. Should have known that athletics are *ancillary* to education, but the two are *concatenated.*

During our first meeting—in the kitchen of his home—a school board president who doubled as a family physician directed me to grill cheese sandwiches on his stove while he grilled *me* on my coaching philosophy. Later, he admitted it was his favorite test for grace under pressure. Got the job, and "Doc" became a lifelong friend.

Fortunately, school leaders usually conduct interviews in more conventional manners.

Dr. Robert Cudney, retired Associate Superintendent of Illinois' Township High School District 214, hired thousands of teachers and coaches. As Personnel Director of one of the larger and more sophisticated districts in the nation for nearly 30 years, Cudney has seen nearly everything.

"I was continually stunned by the number of slipshod applications and weak interviews. Candidates must realize that all interaction—from the very beginning—becomes a presentation of themselves. Misspelled words in carelessly written letters eliminate some candidates from even reaching the interview stage."

Dr. Cudney's recommendations:

- Establish a solid academic foundation.
- Build a collection of references—people familiar with your behaviors, values, and beliefs.
- Develop a strong philosophical base.

- Create a compact and tightly written one-page résumé.
- Emphasize any experience relative to coaching, teaching, or working with people.
- Appreciate the value of maintaining contacts with old coaches, former teachers, and previous principals.
- Submit a clean, concise, grammatically correct, and neatly typed application letter.
- Become an obsessive proofreader.

THE INTERVIEW

Research shows that interviewers often make hiring decisions within the first few minutes. They spend the remainder of the interview searching for evidence to support their decisions, and they seldom change their minds. Because first impressions are so vital, observe the following keys to presenting a positive image.

- Punctuality.
- Neat and appropriate dress.
- Good personal hygiene.
- Genuine smile.
- Direct eye contact.
- Firm handshake.
- Erect body posture.
- Engaging manner of conversing.
- Absence of distracting mannerisms.
- Enthusiasm.

- Projection of sincerity.

Principals continue to interview and make decisions in some schools. But most districts now conduct group interviews or a series of one-on-one discussions with pivotal school personnel.

Districts now favor questioning designed to study candidates' responses to hypothetical cases. Examples:

- How would you react when several of your top athletes are caught vandalizing an opponent's playing field on the eve of the championship football game?

- A teacher informs you that your top pitcher earned a failing grade in her mathematics class; however, she gave a passing mark to keep the athlete eligible for the conference title game. Your response?

- Parents of a freshman football player report a dehumanizing and physically abusive locker room hazing incident in which several seniors humiliated and injured their son. A majority of the varsity players looked on and cheered. Your recommendations?

- How would you greet a prominent local attorney's daughter when she reports for your wrestling team's tryouts?

- We consider alcohol abuse to be the primary problem in our school. As a teacher and coach, what steps will you take to help us combat our most serious concern?

Today's society demands skilled, sensitive, and sturdy people to educate its children. Be prepared with strong philosophical beliefs.

Before interviewing, research school history, philosophies, and traditions as well as community character and culture. This knowledge will help determine your compatibility with the job situation, impress your interviewers, and improve conversational flow.

Dr. Cudney addresses desirable characteristics of candidates for coaching positions by saying, "Coaches, in addition to being strong in the classroom, must have great leadership qualities because of their broad influence and high visibility."

Cudney's experience with candidates for coaching positions shows that some take things for granted. As a former player and present fan with a coaching background, he supports high school sports. And he dislikes stereotyping. But athletes with large-scale egos sometimes expect special consideration for their recognition and awards.

"Athletic success helps," says Cudney, "but go easy

on sounding your own horn. Being an All-American doesn't mean you can get by with sloppy application letters or weak interviews. And it doesn't make you a good coach. Show some humility."

Good schools look for leadership from genuine people. They seek enthusiasm and not a lordly "Here I am" approach. You don't have to be an eloquent articulator—but talk with sincerity. Today's schools are big on ethics, codes of conduct, and coaches who work well with their colleagues.

Can you stand up to pressure?

Are you committed to a career in education?

Do you like young people?

Studying the hiring process brings up the issue of job tenure. How long should a coach remain in one position? The absence of an easy answer, patented formula, or "rule of thumb" leaves us with mere speculation.

The dying breed of *lifers*—those who spend their entire educational careers in coaching (often at the same school)—has almost vanished. Increased mobility and attractive salary schedules at new suburban schools entice coaches to explore different situations. Young people glory in the coaching profession for a few years but soon give it up for something with higher pay, fewer hours, and less emotional trauma.

Don't fall in love with your first job. Attachments to athletes, schools, and communities can become powerful. Beginners often slip into a strong sense of allegiance. Such loyalty, while admirable, should not lead to ignoring better opportunities.

Socializing at clinics and tournaments affords good networking prospects to keep up with X's and O's. And it also alerts coaches to openings in the job market.

School administrators generally agree that "Good people don't stay put very long." Good people tend to be ambitious and enterprising. At the same time, administrators remain wary of *job-hoppers*—those who move too often.

Settle into a job and begin building a positive reputation. Keep your network open and carefully evaluate each opportunity. Develop an eye for potential. As long as you see success in the future, work to strengthen your credentials until the right opportunity comes along.

Smaller districts and communities expect talented and dynamic young people to move toward bigger and better jobs. They may see failure to move ahead as inability to advance and may weaken a coach's credibility.

Evaluate success potential in your job. Avoid "no win" situations.

Countless dramatic turnarounds by coaches stem from

scenery changes. Religious denominations that assign their ministers to congregations—and require frequent relocation—may be on track. They try to match ministers, churches, and communities for maximum success; and then move the ministers before rich relationships erode.

Application letters, résumés, and job interviews are central to successful hiring experiences. You will not get your first job without them. Respect their importance by mastering their essentials. They are valuable vehicles for extending your career progression.

18

Godspeed!

Who doesn't thrill to the color and pageantry of college athletics? Can you resist the spectacle of ancient gridiron rivals colliding on a brilliant autumn afternoon? Or the sizzling insanity that explodes during an NCAA Final Four weekend? We marvel at the majesty of professional athletes' skills. You probably became attracted to the world of sports by watching college and professional games—with their flashy teams, brilliant players, and colorful coaches. And you have dreamed of coaching at a major college or in the professional ranks.

College and professional coaching jobs are scarce, though, and the competition for them is savage. You will likely work with high school boys and girls.

Take heart.

Coaches leave Division I programs every year because they:

- do not win enough.
- are caught cheating.
- detest the dirty tricks of recruiting.
- cannot feel comfortable with the big-time worship of money.

Coaches and managers at the professional level *must* win—while they suffer the outrageous salaries, monumental egos, and insolent attitudes of many of their athletes.

Top college and professional sports have married into show business—where the lust for riches calls the shots.

But high school coaching blends intense competition with positive growth experiences. You can place your brand on a unique style of play—an artistic expression—and also enrich young lives. Help young athletes become better people by teaching them to work together and respect each other. Teach right from wrong. And leave them with lifelong memories.

Few could paint a better picture of a coach than Sharon Randall, a columnist for the *Monterey County Herald* and Scripps Howard News Service. She describes her husband—a California high school basketball coach—by writing:

> He is good at being honest and hardworking and caring—things players ought to see in a coach while learning how to dribble, pass and shoot; how to be fierce on defense, wise with shots; how to keep your mind on the game when your mom's on crack and your dad's in prison and your girlfriend just broke up with you; how to keep your shorts up and your jersey tucked in. Important things like that.

Excluding big-city basketball—where scheming athletes, corrupt coaches, and parasitic street agents are poisoning the game—interscholastic competition attracts followers because of its simplicity and enthusiasm. High school athletes play because they love their game.

As a sportswriter and NBC broadcaster, Brad Holiday covered three World Series, a number of NBA playoffs, and other major sports events. But his sharpest recollections involve high school athletics—his "most special turn-on."

Writing in a St. Louis newspaper about Dike Eddleman of Centralia, the University of Illinois, and the NBA, Holiday quoted some Eddleman reflections. Despite

Dike's Rose Bowl, Olympic Games, and college and professional basketball successes, his greatest thrill came from winning the Illinois state basketball championship in 1942.

Says Holiday, "Interviewing Eddleman was a bigger moment for me than talking with Rogers Hornsby, Rocky Marciano, or Jesse Owens."

In March of 1995—tournament time—Eddleman showed even greater passion for high school sports. After he regained consciousness following a massive heart attack and open-heart surgery, Dike found himself unable to speak. He signaled a doctor and was given a pen and pad of paper. He wrote two words: "Centralia win?"

In this era of permissiveness, societal disrespect, and fewer kids who will run through walls, coaching is not for all people. You need a passionate drive—a fixation—and a ton of mental toughness. You need Don Quixote's innocent enthusiasm and courageous faith to challenge life's windmills—to "run where the brave dare not go."

To maintain sanity in this stress-saturated profession, recognize that:

- there will be winners and losers.
- game officials will make bad calls.
- players will make physical errors and mental mistakes.
- parents will complain.

- fans will criticize.
- the press will be inaccurate and unfair.
- in victory, credit will go to the players.
- in defeat, blame will go to the coach.

That's just the way it is. Understand it and accept it. Do the best you can each day. Sometimes it works out; sometimes it doesn't.

It's not World War III; it's a game. But it's *your* game and it's bigger than those who play and coach. Never allow yourself or any of your players to disgrace its beauty with indifferent effort or poor sportsmanship Be a keeper of the game you teach.

Make doing your best—every time—the essence of your athletic concept. Shoot for perfection; accept excellence. Build a program based on integrity, and dignify your game by promoting decency, sensitivity, and honesty.

Don't mistake these characteristics for signs of weakness. They can be compatible with the most grizzled and battle-scarred warhorses. Coach with *your* personality. Just leave room to care.

Elmer Kelton, the noted Texas novelist, pictures the old-time Western ranchman as one whose "life style gives him an inkling of Heaven and more than his proper share of Hell." His words could describe the high school coach.

Make no mistake. Coaching is a tough, tough business. The well-worn premise that coaches are hired to be fired does not always hold true. But their high profile keeps them vulnerable to the fickle whims of all their publics. Some fear failing enough to board the nonstop carousel of trying to please everybody. Don't do it.

Never allow the thinking of others to control your coaching decisions. If you keep doing all those things that mesh with your convictions—and they still don't want you there—you're a person in the wrong place for you. Be thankful as you move on to something better. Some place that appreciates your values and style.

Zero in on your target and remember Theodore Roosevelt's words: "Far better it is to dare mighty things, to win glorious triumphs, even though checkered by failure, than to take rank with those poor spirits who neither enjoy much nor suffer much, because they live in the gray twilight that knows not victory or defeat."

You've made a good choice. The profession needs you. Young people need you. And *you* need to be a part of something special. You'll never get a huge salary, a million dollar shoe deal, or a high profile TV image. But you have a chance to change the athletic world into a better place to play.

Never say, "I'm ONLY a high school coach." Never. Someday, when you attend a reunion of one of your old teams, you'll see what athletes gain from playing sports. And the role you play in their lives.

Watch a group of middle-aged ex-players from across a broad range of professions and interests come together. Eyes sparkle as they share a camaraderie forged on playing fields of seasons past and bring heartfelt memories back to life. A former player grabs your hand and thanks you for helping make a high school sports experience valuable beyond price. The words reach deep.

Anything that binds individuals around a common cause so tightly must have merit. Sweat, pain, and the ache of a scoreboard defeat are small prices to pay for a wholesome sense of self-worth and a decent set of standards.

What gives me nerve enough to put my thoughts on paper for all who care to see? If somebody, somewhere, finds some small value in these words—then I've repaid a part of what I've taken from others. Borrow anything you can use; and reject the rest. It's your call. You're the Coach.

Johann Wolfgang von Goethe, the German philosopher and writer, inspires us all when we read, "Boldness has genius, power, and magic in it. Whatever you can do, or dream you can can do, begin it."

Mills Lane, the feisty little boxing referee, says it more simply before every big fight: "You've had your instructions. Let's get it on!"

About the Author

Don Schnake graduated from Centralia (Illinois) High School in 1946. He received his BS from Bradley University and an MS from Northern Illinois.

He taught and coached at Illinois high schools in Charleston, Aledo, Vandalia, and Elk Grove Village. In addition to serving as athletic director, his career included head coaching responsibilities in baseball, basketball, cross-country, football and track. His 1972 Elk Grove football team was selected as the Illinois mythical state champion.

During the 1960s, he contributed a regular column to the *Chicago Daily News* as a member of the newspaper's All-State Basketball Board.

In 1987, after 35 years as an educator, Schnake retired and was inducted into the Illinois Football Coaches Hall of Fame.

In 1992, he authored the award-winning biography *TROUT: The Old Man and the Orphans*. This is his second book publication.

Index

A
academics 80, 100
Agase, Alex 20
Allen, George 20
Allen, Phog 20
Ameche, Alan 41
assistant coaches 21, 52, 103-108, 118, 156

B
Baker, Merv 20
Bee, Clair 20
Bell, Taylor 109
Berry, Raymond 41
booster clubs 139
Borders, Ila 160
Broyles, Frank 20
Bryant, Bear 20, 32, 155
Byrnes, Robert 111

C
Chaney, John 47
Changnon, Stan 20
Chicago Bulls 48
coaching by committee 105
coaching clinics 20, 38-39
Combes, Harry 19
communication 35, 72, 81, 90, 97, 152, 166
Corray, Fred 45
credibility 35, 40, 62, 80, 96, 105, 147, 178
Csonka, Larry 41
Cudney, Robert 173, 176

D
Danielson, Gary 88
Davis, Pamela 161
demonstration 81-83
discipline 26, 58, 59, 86, 114, 165
distributive practice 86
Dorr, Dave 111
Durocher, Leo 152

E
Eddleman, Dike 183-184
Eveland, Ernie 20
explanation 63, 81-82

F
Flynn, Brendan 21
Frisk, Bob 68

G

Gagliardi, John 32
Gaters, Dorothy 164
Goethe, Johann Wolfgang von 187
goodwill enhancement 140
Grams, Ken 166-167
Griese, Bob 42

H

Halas, George 32
Harmon, Pat 45
Hayes, Woody 20, 32, 88, 123
head coaches 103-107, 156
Hickey, Eddie 20
Holiday, Brad 183
Holman, Nat 20
Holtz, Lou 20
Hornsby, Rogers 184
Huxley, Thomas 59

I

Iba, Henry 20

K

Kanter, Dee 126
Karhu, Milo 89-90
Kelton, Elmer 185
Kiick, Jim 41
Kintner, Gay 20
Knight, Bob 111, 123
Krysh, Marcia 165, 167
Kurland, Max 36

L

Lane, Mills 187
Lansing, Alfred 51
leadership 13, 51, 98, 107, 176-177
Leahy, Frank 83
Levy, Marv 144
liability 36, 64,
Lichtenfeldt, John 98
Lincoln, Abraham 144
Little League 31
Lombardi, Vince 30, 32, 68
losing 65-66

M

Mackey, John 41
Marciano, Rocky 184
Marino, Dan 42
Matte, Tom 41
McCartney, Bill 68
McDaniel, Heather 126
McGuire, Al 90
McGuire, Frank 20
McGuire, Kay 78
McKay, John 21
Melchiorre, Gene 20
mentoring 40
Meyer, Ray 20
Mooney, Sam 46
Moore, Lenny 41
Morris, Mercury 41

O
Oldfield, James 36-37
Ortiz-Del Valle, Sandhi 126
Owens, Jesse 184
P
parent clubs 132
Parseghian, Ara 21
Paterno, Joe 21
Peddy, Larry 119
people-skills 36, 105, 137
philosophy 20, 29-34, 47, 97, 111, 132-133
players' coach 55
practice 42, 72, 77, 79-90
Pratt, George 20, 39
program 51-53, 56, 137
Prine, John 72
public relations 35, 137, 140-141
publics 140-141, 153, 171, 186
Q
Quixote, Don 184
R
Randall, Sharon 182
Ray, Alden 111
recruiting 134, 145, 147-150
recruiting analysts 150
repetition 45, 47, 81, 83-84
respect 26, 35, 37, 52-53, 75, 78, 80, 83, 96, 98-99, 105, 108, 114, 118, 121-123, 126

Riley, Pat 47
Robinson, Eddie 21, 32
Robinson, John 21
Rockne, Knute 72
Roosevelt, Theodore 186
Royal, Darrell 21
Rupp, Adolph 20, 47
S
Schembechler, Bo 21
Schnake, Chuck 140-141
Scholten, Peggy 132, 165-166
self-improvement programs 38
separation 97
Shackleton, Ernest 52
Schula, Don 41
Smith, Marvin 114-115
Spoonhour, Charlie 54
Spurgeon, Lowell 110
staff meetings 32, 106
Stagg, Amos 32
Stanley, Dolph 20
Steinbeck, John 66
street agents 149, 183
stress 99, 184
style 29, 32-33, 42, 45, 47
summer camps 54, 131, 150
Symington, Stuart 138
T
talent scouts 150
Tasker, Ralph 46-47, 55

Thoman, Bus 115
Thomas, Duster 20, 43
Title IX 126, 159-160, 162, 166-168
training rules 59, 61
Trout, A.L. 18-19, 44-47, 55-56, 70-71, 98-99, 110-111, 118, 124, 142-144, 153-154
Tucker, Steve 130

U

Unitas, John 41
unity 52, 56, 75, 130, 156
Unruh, Paul 20
U.S. Supreme Court 61

V

visualization 38

W

Walsh, Bill 21
Warner, Pop 32
Warren, William 75
Waugh, Maury 67
Wilkinson, Bud 21
Wollstonecraft, Mary 136
Wooden, John 21, 44, 81
Wyatt, Bowden 21

Z

Zuppke, Bob 110

ORDER FORM

Thank you for reading *COACHING: 101*.

If you would like additional copies, please use the form below.

••

Please send _____ copies of
COACHING 101: Guiding the High School Athlete and Building Team Success
@ 12.95 per copy _____

Also available from *Richview Press*:
TROUT: The Old Man and the Orphans
@ 11.95 per copy _____

Sales Tax-Illinois residents add .97 per book _____

Shipping 1.50 per book _____

Total Amount _____

Ship to: (Please print)

Name: _____

Address: _____

City, State, Zip: _____

Phone: _____-_____-_____

Make checks payable to *Richview Press*

Send to:
Richview Press
P.O. Box 92174, Elk Grove Village, IL 60009-2174
Tel. 847-437-3417